Hope and Healing for My Wounded and Broken Heart

by Rachel A Bollinger

To the readers who purchased this volume, thank you.

Dedication

Dedicated to Bettye O. Fulcher
Faithful friend for over fifty years

HOPE AND HEALING FOR MY WOUNDED AND BROKEN HEART

TABLE OF CONTENTS

INTRODUCTION

"I will give you hidden treasures, riches stored in secret places, so that you may know that I am the LORD, the God of Israel, who summons you by name."
Isaiah 45:3

Finding Hidden Treasure

Have you ever had a moment when a song, the scent of a particular recipe or a picture touched deeply on emotions you had forgotten were there? That's what happened to me the day I went up to the bonus room in my house. I have created a cozy private space that I go to when I want to spend time with the Lord, read or write. I start my mornings by the window sitting on the big brown La-Z-Boy love seat. I curl up with my Bible, my journal, and my prayer list book. Across the room in the corner is my desk where the words hit the page. A printer on one corner, the laptop on the other and my big monitor in the middle. This room also serves as a guest room and craft room. I recently added my electric piano. When I need a break from typing and thinking, I wander over to the piano and entertain myself for a few minutes. It was into this room that I brought from the attic four large plastic storage boxes that held memorabilia as well as several plastic cases of pictures.

I started writing over twenty years ago and had a small book of poetry and short articles published in 2018. However, I hadn't written anything for several years and was questioning if I was supposed to continue writing. After attending a retreat that involved some soul searching I came away knowing I was supposed to continue and "Write it down for the honor and glory of God." I commissioned a large wooden sign bearing those words and hung it on the wall in my cozy space. The sign was always a reminder that when the time was right, I would write again. The time was right.

Even if you are unfamiliar with or do not believe the story the Bible tells, I hope you will come along with me as I share my journey; how I learned to reject the lies that had wounded and broken my heart and how my relationship deepened with the only one who had promised to heal my heart – Psalm 147:3 "He heals the broken hearted and binds up their wounds."

I unsnapped the lid of the first large clear plastic container, pulled out a large navy-blue book, and rubbed my hand across the gold letters on the cover that spelled "Scrapbook." A gold tasselled cord held the pages together between the covers. Sometimes a scrapbook will have been carefully curated with neatly written captions and cute little stickers and tell a special story. However, this scrapbook told me, "You found a place where things you wanted to keep were just pasted on my pages in no particular order." When I gently opened it, memories from the 90's, when I had struggled with a debilitating health problem, appeared. I'll be sharing all about that time later. The get-well cards and the notes of encouragement I had received during those years were also pasted on those pages. As I flipped through them and re-read the cards, I saw the faces of many people from over 30 years ago who had reached out to me with love and encouragement. There were also some birthday cards and little notes from nieces and nephews. Tears trickled down my face as I paged though that scrapbook.

I lifted out the next book, also a scrapbook. This one was much harder to look through. It contained only one kind of card or letter: sympathy cards and letters received after the sudden loss of my first husband, Wayne. I was immediately transported back to that terrible day in 1997. Even as I remembered the pain, I found comfort when again I saw the names of friends and family who during that time of grief had offered words of love and encouragement to me that brought back beautiful memories of my husband.

After Wayne's death I spent some time living in Colorado. Digging down to the bottom of the box, I found a small book that contained the goodbye notes and cards from my 50th birthday/going away party when I moved from Colorado to North Carolina. Holding those items helped refresh my memory about the good times that had gotten lost in the pain of the hard and bad times. Memory lane had been a good thing.

Tears, laughter, struggle, and triumph were represented in the twenty-six years of journals that filled the second container. Those journals made up my personal book of Psalms. In them I lamented and I laughed. I earnestly prayed and I recorded the joys and the tears as through the years there were weddings, funerals, and grandchildren. There was moving, job changes, and health crises recorded. (Like the time that … But I've saved that story for later.) There were questions for God and thanksgiving as well. There were promises made and promises broken. Those journals reminded me of God's faithfulness.

The third container was large and held 33 workbooks from each of the formal Bible studies I had participated in since 1998. I wondered, *What did I really learn from all of those?*" As I looked at the titles, I was reminded that I had learned about Gideon, Elijah, Jonah, and Esther to name a few. My relationship with my Heavenly Father had grown as I became more acquainted with Him through each study. As I continued my journey what I had previously learned became clear.

The fourth and final container was also plastic with a snap on lid but was quite a bit smaller. It looked like a filing cabinet drawer and held copies of all the articles I had ever written. In it I found a book proposal from twenty years ago that, with just a few tweaks, perfectly described this book. I was reminded that I'd been on this writing journey for many years. I also found Dad's genealogy in that container. I had no idea how that genealogy was going to give me answers to many of my questions about my relationship with my dad, but it piqued my curiosity for sure.

One of the tasks I had carried out during the COVID shutdown had been to organize all my pictures. They now lived in four large *Photo Storage Keeper* containers neatly sorted and labelled. Seeing pictures of my birthday party when I was five made me smile. The look of fear on my face in the picture of me when I was performing with the group on stage at Bible School made me sad. It was like riding a roller-coaster of emotions as I quickly scanned the decades of my life.

Why had I gone to the attic to retrieve those containers? It was because of a journal entry I made on January 14, 2023.

That entry read, "Woke up this morning singing in my head and heart –

All my life you have been faithful.
All my life you have been so, so good.
With every breath that I am able
I will sing of the goodness of God.[1]

The entry continued as I recorded my memories of the wounds and heartbreak I had encountered. I knew that He had faithfully been there as different events and many

---

[1] Johnson, 2019, Goodness of God, Bethel Music, https://www.youtube.com/watch?v=n0FBb6hnwTo

relationships had wounded and broken my heart. The information in those containers, the help of a counselor, my Bible, family, and friends were what God used to heal my wounded and broken heart.

Have you ever been with family or friends when you started discussing old memories? Someone recounts an event, and you think, *that's not how I remember it.* This book is about my journey as my old memories were confronted with what had really happened. The good that had gotten lost in the bad memories. The journey was long and hard, but it brought peace and joy as truth triumphed over lies again and again. Buckle up and join me.

CHAPTER ONE – WHO TOLD YOU THAT?

I love those who love me, and those who seek me diligently find me.
Proverbs 8:17

Taking The First Step

One Sunday morning at the end of January 2023, the name and dates of the next women's Bible study flashed on the screen in the worship center at my church - Breaking Free From Body Shame.[2] I wondered if it was really possible to break free? My friend and I had discussed this topic many times on our walks. For years I had written about it in my journals. Was I ready to tackle this topic? I saw that the study was going to be on Monday night for six weeks. *Oh good,* I thought, *since I am already taking part in a Monday night study I am off the hook.* But every week when the notice about the study flashed on the screen, I knew in my heart it was time to deal with the shame, and I should go. When I talked to the ladies in my current study, they encouraged me to take a break from them and attend the classes. I was ready

---

[2] Jess Connolly, Breaking Free from Body Shame (Grand Rapids, Zondervan, 2021)

– but I wasn't. It took everything I had to make myself go to class the first night.

As I stood in front of the mirror getting ready, the voice inside my head said, *"Look at your face. If you go tonight, you are going to be embarrassed."* The voice was right, I was embarrassed. I had just recently been to the dermatologist for some spots on my face and this time instead of burning them off the doctor had prescribed some chemotherapy cream. It had been applied to the suspicious areas and would only kill cancer cells and potentially cancerous cells. I was experiencing all of the possible side effects; peeling, irritation, swelling, itching and tenderness. There were red scaly blotches all across my nose and parts of my face. The voice continued, *"You know you don't want to go."* Right again. *"You know you shouldn't even need to be there."* I believed that too. *"How many diets have you already tried?"* More than I could count. *"How many miles of walking have you logged?"* Again, more than I could count. *"You should already be over this."* I had told myself that many, many times. *"You are 71 years old. What makes you think this time will be different?"* I didn't have an answer to that question but was going to try to find it. The idea of "body shame" resonated deeply. The fight against body shame started when I was ten with an event I'll share later. My first official diet didn't start until I was in my early twenties. However, after that my weight was up and down and I was either getting ready for a diet, on a diet, or quitting a diet. No matter how much weight I lost the body shame never went away.

There was only one reason I could walk into the room that night and join the thirty other women who were there. I had **HOPE!** I was ready to learn how to love the body God gave me even if it didn't look the way I wanted it to or how I believed others expected it to look.

Hal Lindsey says, "Man can live about forty days without food, about three days without water, about eight minutes without air…but only for one second without hope."[3] The Merriam-Webster dictionary definition of hope is: "to cherish a desire with anticipation: to want something to happen or to be true."[4] I cherished the desire to be free of shame and I still had hope. I didn't know that body shame was just a symptom of a much more insidious problem. I didn't realize it, but God had been preparing me for that class.

The voice inside my head continued to taunt me as I arrived for the first night of class. *"You're going to be so embarrassed,"* it reminded me again. *"You are going to be the oldest one there,"* it whispered. And of course it said, *"I can't believe you don't already have victory over this."* The load of guilt and shame weighed heavily as I entered the room. I found my name and took my seat with Carley, my table leader. In a few minutes, the other six ladies joined us. I could tell as I looked at their sweet young faces that they too were weighed down. (The voice had been correct about one thing – I was at least twice as old as most of them.) We introduced ourselves and shared parts of our stories. Childhood sexual abuse, difficult marriages, and wanting to be married but believing they were damaged goods were some of the shame-inducing events that we shared. We already felt a bit better because we knew that at least we weren't in this alone.

Arriving at this part of my story and reflecting on those weeks, I decided that I could best explain what I had learned by writing a letter to Carley who had been my table leader. *Dear Carley,*

---

[3] https://www.goodreads.com/author/quotes/11197.Hal_Lindsey
[4] https://www.merriam-webster.com/hope

8

I'm so glad that you were my table leader for those weeks of the Women's Bible Study. (I had gotten to know you as we chatted each Sunday morning at your post outside the Children's Ministry Hall.) You were such an encourager as you had a word of encouragement on a sticky note for each of us every Monday night. All of mine are still pasted in the front of my workbook. I was able to attend every week and the discussions about the homework with you and the other six ladies were really helpful.

*We covered a lot of territory those six weeks. Before the study when I thought about my body I only thought about my physical appearance, and I hated it. But we spent time talking about how our bodies are so much more than just our physical appearance. Our sense of touch, taste, sight, hearing, thinking, walking, sitting and more are all part of our bodies. Internalizing this helped me take the first step toward healing. The homework the first week had us look at Psalm 139 that declared God's knowledge of us. He knows us when we get up and when we sit down. He knows what we are thinking and what we will say before we even say it. The many times I had read that chapter I had missed something important. David said in verse 14 that he would **praise** God because he was fearfully and wonderfully made. I hadn't noticed the element of praise in that verse before. David wasn't praising God because he had an impressive body. He wasn't praising the creation. He was praising the Creator.*

An illustration I had read came to mind and helped me think differently about my body. If I bought a picture at a yard sale for $20.00 and later found out it was a Rembrandt, my understanding of the value of the painting would change drastically. I realized that I had been seeing and treating my body like a $20.00 yard sale item when in fact it was a God created original. Now I could truly praise God for my body and all its amazing abilities and functions. My fearfully and *wonderfully made body became a reason for joy, not for shame. It would take time for this information to truly renew my mind, but it was a start.*

As the weeks went by, we were reminded from Genesis 1-3 that God had ascribed value and worth to His creation. At the same time the enemy (Satan) convinced humans for the first time that God wasn't trustworthy. Any feelings of shame we had about our bodies and about God not being trustworthy were exposed for the lies they were. We were getting to the heart of the problem, and I was more ready than ever to keep going.

I loved week three when we were introduced to the idea of resting from thinking of our bodies as a project that needed to be fixed. We didn't need one more diet, more time walking, or more exercises to keep us from being ashamed of our bodies. We were getting it. I know I was starting to understand the lies I had believed that had created the feeling of being "not enough."

Do you remember how I groaned out loud when our study leader, Merideth, announced that we weren't going to have table discussion the fourth week? Instead, we were going to spend the time alone reflecting on Psalm 23. I disliked that type of activity because in the past I never believed I had learned anything from them. With a less than willing heart I found a chair away from everyone and opened my Bible.

This time it was different. I heard God say to me, "Rachel, I have always known your heart." A little bit of healing took place in that moment. By the time we were called back to our tables, I had two pages of notes. As I had read Psalm 23, that I knew by heart, I connected with it in a new way. I had seen a reason to worship Him as my shepherd. I saw that He leads me in paths of righteousness for His name's sake, not mine. I saw the valley of the shadow of death as the world I live in, and I didn't have to fear it because I don't have to conform to it. With new insight I thought about how the Shepherd's rod is used to fight the enemy, and how His staff can get me out of trouble; how there is anointing oil that gives healing, and how an overflowing cup represents abundant life. The promise of dwelling in the house of the Lord forever ended the passage and refocused my mind that life is not all about the here and now, I had heaven to look forward to.

Wow! Not only had He seen me right then in my class, but I also realized that He had known my heart all the years I struggled in my first marriage, with my weight, with feelings of being inadequate, and not good enough. He had known I wanted to please him. He knew me, He loved me, He was waiting for me, and He was working with me. He knew me in the past and knew me that night. As I went back to our table, He knew that I was ready to unpack the lies about not being worthy of love that were buried in my mind and heart. Weeks five and six were group times of reflection and some prayer and praise time confirming my need to continue on the journey to freedom and healing.

Thanks Carley, for your faithful leadership and encouragement during those weeks. It has been fun to stay in touch and see all that God has done in your life, including getting to attend your wedding to Micah!

Love you, Rachel

Compassionate Listening

During the six weeks of Bible Study there had been three licensed counselors available on site every Monday night. As the weeks continued, pain from some old wounds had surfaced and I knew I needed outside help to make sense of them. I went to Dawn, one of the counselors, and told her I needed to make an appointment with her. She graciously put me on her waiting list. My first appointment was May 25,

2023. I arrived at her office ready to get started. This letter explains what I learned that first day.

Dear Dawn,

I will always be grateful for that first hour I got to spend with you. I told you about an incident that happened when I was eleven or twelve. It involved a family member and wounded me deeply and I had never told anyone about it. The tears began to fall as I shared the story and the pain with you. You listened intently without judgement. Your response was no different than if I had told you I had a milkshake on the way over to your office. It was an event that had happened and there was instant relief from sharing it. You said, "Shame can't survive being spoken. Shame needs three things to survive: secrecy, silence, and judgement." The silence had been broken, the secret had been shared, I judged it as the lie it was so that shame didn't survive our first session.

We talked more and I shared more of my life. Some things I just shared as facts and some things I shared brought tears. The ones that brought tears were covered in shame. I began to recognize that the shame I had carried all these years had not been mine to carry. As our time ran out that day, you confirmed what I had been figuring out in class. You said, "Over the years, you have internalized some lies that have led you to believe you are not enough," You were right. I believed I had not been a good enough mother, or wife, or employee – and on and on the list went. But, most of all I believed I had not been a good enough Christ follower. In other words, I haven't been perfect in any of those roles, so I was a failure. You assured me that we were going to find the answers I was looking for.

Thanks for your help, Dawn. I'm looking forward to our next session.

Gratefully, Rachel

Searching for Truth

As I continued to see Dawn over the next several months, I could see that something wasn't adding up. I knew that John 8:32 said, "you shall know the truth and the truth shall make you free," but I hadn't been living in freedom. If I hadn't been believing and living the truth of God's Word, then there is only one thing that could mean – I had been living and believing a lie. A lie always has the intent to deceive. Who had been deceiving me? I found more truth as I continued to see Dawn.

My next clue came from a sermon Joseph, one of our campus pastors, preached in July of 2023. What I have written here I have shared with Joseph in person.

Dear Pastor Joseph,

It was just a few months after I attended the Breaking Free from Body Shame class that I heard you preach your sermon titled, "Trust the Process"[5]. Using II Samuel 24 you reminded us about a time in King David's life when God allowed him to fail so that he could be fruitful in seasons to come.

In this sermon you used an illustration that resonated with me. You said a grave digger and an archaeologist both use a shovel. One buries; one uncovers. I realized that the grave digger, Satan, had been burying me in shame. The archaeologist, Jesus, was going to help me uncover the truth. I was going to start "trusting the process." I was going to be willing to experience the pain of remembering and do the hard work so I could experience the healing and freedom God intends for me.

Thanks, Joseph, for your faithful exposition of God's Word.

Gratefully, Rachel

---

[5] https://mercycharlotte.com/sermons/5210/

Trust The Process

I loved the idea of a process. That's how God had wired my brain. I had developed a process for almost every job I ever had. Having a process made life easier and more predictable for me. I thought, *I wonder what process an archaeologist uses? Will a similar process work for me?* After a quick Google search, I was delighted to discover that it was exactly what I needed. Even though I hadn't written the process down I later realized that I had been following the steps. I had no idea it would take so long. I had been seeing Dawn for a year when I decided it was time to start putting what I was learning into a book.

Step one for the archaeologist was to name the questions that needed to be answered and develop a research design, outline the project's goals, methods, and expected outcomes. That's how I started, too.

My questions were:

1.) *How did I get to be 71 and still be worried about body shame?*

2.) *Why did I think I hadn't been good enough?*

I developed my research design unintentionally. The week after Joseph's sermon, at the end of July 2023 while traveling, I left my phone in a restroom at the airport. It had not been turned into the lost and found before it was the time for our flight. I used my husband's phone, suspended my service, and boarded the plane. (Side note, after being single for over twelve years I had remarried in June of 2010.) I wondered to myself, *What in the world am I going to do for the next three hours with no phone?* I found a small notepad and a pencil in my purse, and I created a very basic timeline. I had lived in seven different states during my seven decades, so I started with that. The first line said, October 1, 1951 – September 1969 – Hammond, Indiana. By the time we reached our destination I had completed a rough draft that included the dates and places where I had lived and also all the places I had worked.

Because I had an affinity for spreadsheets, when I got home I entered the information from those slips of paper into a spreadsheet. That became the outline for my project. Decade by decade I used that information as I searched for the answers to all my who, why, when, where, and how questions. The ultimate goal was to find healing for my heart and mind.

Not only did I love spreadsheets, but I also loved manila folders. (One of my favorite jobs was when I worked for an office products company; Pens, pencils, and notebooks, too, OH MY!) The method I used for the collection of data that couldn't be entered on a spreadsheet was to create a manila folder for each decade, as well as one for my dad and one for my mom. Those folders went with me for days as I moved from room to room in my house. As I remembered things I wrote them on and in the folders. Sometimes I took them with me in the car just in case I remembered something important while I was out. For several weeks my mind was constantly busy replaying my life decade by decade. I was fleshing out the information that was on my timeline. I was on my way; I had my questions, and I knew how I planned to find the answers. I was ready for step two.

Step two for the archaeologist was to get funding and permits. No funding was needed but I did need a publisher. In 2008 my first book *Drawing From The Well*[6] had been published. I contacted them to see if they would be interested in publishing this book. They said they would. That item was checked off my list.

---

6 Rachel Bollinger, Drawing from the Well, (Fernandina Beach, FL, Left Hand Publishers, 2018)

Next on the list for the archaeologist was site choice. I already knew the sites I needed to excavate were my heart and my mind. That's where the wounds and heartbreak lived and that's also where the healing would happen.

I collected more background information that hadn't been in my containers. The online searches I did yielded birth and death certificates for some of my parents' relatives. I also found information about the culture during my parents' early years. I looked at maps of my hometown to remind myself where my schools, my church and my friends' homes had been found.

The next big step for the archaeologist was to start digging. I had my manila folders set up to store and record my finds. The layers of my dig were my decades, and I was meticulous about recording what wounds I found in each layer. I had a small sticker printer that I used to take pictures of the larger artifacts that wouldn't fit in the folders. I applied the stickers to the front of each corresponding manila folder.

Processing and analysing was hard work and took a lot of time. When I had first started putting words on the page, I had assumed I was writing the book. I had been working on it for several months before I realized what I had really been doing was curating my information. I had been summarizing all that I had collected and learned. Because I wasn't writing an autobiography or memoir, I had more information than I needed to share. I wasn't going to write about every detail of my seventy plus years. (Wow, it makes me cringe to even think about having to read that.)

I understood that I would only need to share information that was relevant to three things:

1.) The lies I had believed that led to shame.

2.) The truth I had learned that exposed and healed the shame.

3.) How my mind had been involved with both the lies that had wounded, and the truth that led to healing.

As you read the next chapters, I pray that you too may find hope and healing for your wounds and heartbreaks. But first I need to talk to Jesus.

So What?

Dear Jesus,

Thank you that in response to my crying out to You and wanting freedom from my shame, you answered. Through the book we read and the other ladies in my class You reminded me that I had never been alone in my struggle and that I wasn't bad because I struggled. In Genesis 3:17 You told Adam and Eve "Because you (sinned)…all your life You will struggle." (NLT) You told Your disciples in John 16:33 "…in this world you will have trouble…"

Not only have You answered my specific prayer You have shown me so many other areas that needed freedom from shame. I have learned so much about You and who You are through this journey. It has not been about writing a book; it has been about recording the work You are doing in my life so that others may know that You can do a work in theirs too. I pray right now for anyone who is reading this book that they will only see You and Your offer of healing as they continue to read.

I love You, Lord, and thank You for loving me.
Amen

CHAPTER TWO —LET THE DIGGING BEGIN

Trust God's character more than you trust your circumstances.
Angie Smith

The Most Important Thing About Me

Would you look at how that diamond is sparkling? I thought to myself as I sat in the living room moving my hand around letting my engagement ring catch the sunlight. As I continued to enjoy the moment my mind started doing its thing – taking an ordinary moment and making it a God moment. I thought about how the light hadn't just hit one facet of the diamond, but it hit the diamond as a whole and that is what gave it the sparkle, brilliance, and beauty. Then I thought about how all of the facets were a permanent part of the diamond and no one facet could be removed. The amount of sparkle and shine was dependent on a few things; the amount of light, the kind of light available, and how clean the ring is. Then came my God moment – I thought, *Just like the facets of my diamond all of God's attributes are always present.* In my mind I then pictured a large diamond with beams of light flowing from it. Each beam represented an attribute of God. A.W. Tozer wrote, "An attribute of God is whatever God has in any way revealed as being true of Himself,"[7] His love, faithfulness, omniscience, holiness, justice, and mercy, to name a few

---

7 A. W. Tozer, The Knowledge of the Holy (New York: Harper One, 1961) pg. 12

were all inseparable. Tozer explained, "An attribute is not a part of God. It is *how* God is."[8] He is kind, He is love, He is merciful, etc. In other words, He does not cease being love when He is just. He can't be mean or unkind. His love for me didn't ever change based on how the light was shining at that moment. All the attributes of God are just like the facets of my ring, always there and inseparable.

That led me to think about another quote from A.W. Tozer. "What comes into our minds when we think about God is the most important thing about us."[9] He went on to say, "Only after an ordeal of painful self-probing are we likely to discover what we actually believe about God."[10] The excavation was painful as I probed. I found out what I had believed to be true about God had been incomplete and/or inaccurate through all the decades of my life. God gently and thoroughly brushed away the errors and increased my knowledge of Him as I moved ahead.

One of the ways that knowledge increased was by being reminded that not only was it important to learn about God's attributes, for example His sovereignty and His omnipresence, but it was also important to understand about His names. God has many names that represent His attributes. In scripture El Elyon: The God Most High represents His sovereignty, and His omnipresence is seen in his name El Roi; The God Who Sees. As I pondered that I thought about my name – *Rachel*. I started my life as *Rachel*, the daughter of Albert and Louise. At the same time, I was *Rachel*, Phil, and Tim's sister. I was a granddaughter and also a niece. Over the years I would add many more, friend, wife, mother, and grandmother to name a few. But what does it mean to be *Rachel*, daughter of God – the God who sees, who heals and

---

[8] Ibid. pg. 16
[9] Ibid. pg. 1
[10] Ibid, pg. 2

sustains? What would it mean to allow God's daughter to supersede all of these other roles I had taken on? As the excavation continued, I was going to find out.

Not only did I need to understand more about God, but I also needed to understand the role Satan had played in my life. Because I also had incomplete and inaccurate information about him, particularly the level of deception he can create, so the conclusions I reached over the years had been flawed. So that was the next place I needed to dig.

More Dawn Insights

Dear Dawn,

In one of our sessions, as I was sitting comfortably on the sofa facing you, we were discussing how Satan had gotten into my mind. You explained, "Satan tells you a lie. You believe the lie and make it a rule for your life. Then when you break the rule, Satan throws it back at you and shames you for not keeping it. Shame is focused on self and says I'm bad, while guilt says I did something wrong." I pondered this information for a long time after that session. I still didn't think I was important enough for Satan to specifically tell me anything.

Then I remembered the verse in Ephesians 2:2 that said Satan was "the prince of the power of the air." (ESV) He was the authority on earth and had demons and evil spirits under his control. He was a created being who couldn't be everywhere at once, so he had lots of helpers. I recognized the truth that Satan was the father of lies so anything that wasn't truth was a lie from him, and he didn't have to "personally" whisper it in my ear. You were helping me learn to be a good "lie detector."

Gratefully, Rachel

The Father of Lies

My heavenly Father, the archaeologist of my life, helped me use my lie detector skills to uncover my incomplete/inaccurate view of Satan. "The Devil is a sly old fox. If I could catch him, I'd put him in a box. Lock him up and throw away the key, for all the tricks he had played on me," were the lyrics of a Sunday School song I learned as a child that had given me very inaccurate and incomplete information about Satan. I knew there was a devil, but I didn't believe that I was important enough to be a threat to him. I didn't understand what it said in I Peter 5:8-9 "…your adversary the devil prowls around like a roaring lion, seeking someone to devour."

He wasn't a sly old fox I could put in a box. He was my enemy. In her book *Upon Waking* Jackie Hill Perry said that being ignorant of the devil's schemes was actually one of his schemes.

"You won't resist an enemy you forget exists. You won't fight a devil you don't believe is real. After you open the blinds and let the light in, you will see that flesh and blood has never been the real enemy. There are rulers, authorities, "cosmic powers over this present darkness: and "spiritual forces of evil" with concentrated hate toward the people of God (Eph 6:12)."[11]

In John Mark Comer's book *Live No Lies,* he quotes from Tim Chaddick's book *The Truth About Lies,* "our fight with the devil is first and foremost a fight to take back control of our minds from their captivity to lies and liberate them with the weapon of truth."[12]

---

[11] Jackie Hill Perry, *Upon Waking* (Brentwood, TN, B&H Publishing, 2023) page 92

[12] John Mark Comer, *Live No Lies* (WaterBrook, 2021) page 7)

I had known the devil was real. I just hadn't understood how he had been active in my life. As my excavation project continued, I learned more and what I learned led to healing. Satan had weaponized his lies, and I learned how to fight back is to weaponize the truth just like Jesus did when Satan tempted Him in Matthew chapter four.

That Thing Called Shame

As I remembered my journal entry where I had listed all of the ways God had been faithful to me over the seven decades of my life, I found the common denominator for each event had been shame. What did it mean that God had been faithful during those events that were filled with shame? As I dug further the answer to that question became clear.

Of all the things I read about shame, Dr Thompson's explanation of shame in his book "*The Soul of Shame,* resonated with me best. "Shame's presence is ubiquitous and inserts itself into the genetic material of the human storytelling endeavor. One way to envision shame is as a personal attendant. Imagine that you have a completely devoted attendant attuned to every sensation, image, feeling, thought and behavior you have. However, imagine that your shame attendant's intention is not good, is not to care for you but rather to infuse nonverbal and verbal elements of judgement into every moment of your life. The word *attendant* at first may seem counterintuitive, as it usually applies to someone who has our best interests in mind. But this is how shame works, a wolf disguised in sheep's clothing. Hence, our shame attendant appears in language, feelings, sensations, and images that may on the surface seem acceptable, common, and normal, but its purpose is anything but helpful."[13] My personal shame attendant had been very busy my whole life. All my digging exposed him and his lies.

How My Mind Works

If I was going to fight the devil and take back control of my mind, I needed to understand how it worked. The next layer of my dig took me to more of the book, *The Soul of Shame,*[14] suggested to me by Dawn. I can't tell you how many hours I spent digging and devouring the information presented in its pages. One of the things that fascinated me in this book was information about the nine functions of my brain. Using those nine functions as a guideline I did some web searches and was able to dumb it down to my level. I knew about the brain stem and the right brain, left brain and prefrontal cortex, but I didn't know what each part did nor how they all needed to work together for our minds to be what Dr. Thompson calls "integrated."

The first function made so much sense, **consciousness** – being aware. My general level of awareness of what I was sensing, perceiving, feeling, thinking, and doing at any given moment. The dictionary definition of mind is, "the seat of awareness, thought, volition, feeling, and memory."[15] The trick was to pay attention to what I paid attention to. I thought about how many times I had been driving and arrived at my destination without remembering the drive; not being aware of what I was aware of at its finest.

The **vertical** function of our brain develops from the bottom up. The hindbrain is the survival part of the brain and includes the stem and amygdala. It was described as the survival part of the brain that controlled fight or flight. The

---

[13] Curt Thompson, *The Soul of Shame*, (Downers Grove, IL: IVP Books, 2015) pg. 92

[14] Thompson, The Soul of Shame

[15] https://www.oed.com/dictionary/mind

midbrain is the feeling part where emotions are experienced. Last is the forebrain that is the thinking part of the brain. It controls reasoning, problem solving, etc.

The **horizontal** portion of my brain referred to the right and left hemispheres. I knew about them from all the talk about people being right or left brained. However, I didn't know that the right hemisphere grew faster than the left for the first eighteen to twenty-four months of life. I didn't know all that happened in those two hemispheres. I found out that the right side is the center of visuo-spatial orientation, nonverbal communication, and emotion while the left side is the center of much of our language, logical, linear, and literal thought processes. As the two sides start working together it's the left brains job to make sense of the information the right brain is sending it.

The next function of my brain listed was **memory**. There were two types of memory discussed, implicit and explicit. After some further research I was able to determine that my implicit memory operated unconsciously and without intentional effort. Explicit memory involved conscious recall. Implicit memory influenced my behavior and decision making without me realizing its impact. One example that encompasses both types was tying my shoes. It took explicit memory to learn the skill but eventually it became implicit memory, automatic and required little conscious thought.

Narrative happened as my mind developed and I eventually tried to make sense of my life. I took input from my awareness of my conscious, vertical, horizontal, and memory functions as I began to tell my story. Dr Thompson says that most of the narrative information was nonverbal and nonconscious and was also highly influenced by my most intimate attachment relationships.[16] This would be important information when I excavated my first decade.

Next in the list came **state.** Neuroscientists now know that how my brain fires is directly related to what is happening around me. My state of mind fluctuates throughout my day. When I sit down to play the piano my brain would fire differently than when I am having an argument with someone.

The **interpersonal**. "For all that convinces me that my mind is limited to "me," the truth remains that a great deal of my mind's activity is wrapped up with thinking about or interacting with other people's minds. ...in other words, there is rarely anything I do that is not either influencing or being influenced by our minds. And shame has no trouble swimming in the current that is constantly flowing between us."[17]

Temporal is the capacity I had to reflect on my past and my future and give meaning to the things I remembered; also, to understand that I had a beginning and I will have an end.

All of the nine functions Dr Thompson shared were from a book, *Mindsight*, by Daniel Siegel. This last word was one that Daniel Siegel made up to refer to the process of managing all the other eight functions simultaneously. The word was **transpirational**. Dr Thompson ends the section this way, "the overall implication is that to be aware of the activity of one's mind is a matter of hard work. ...if we are not attending to them shame will have a much easier time wreaking havoc on all of them."[18] I don't know about you, but I needed a nap and a Tylenol by the time I finished that section.

---

[16] Thompson, The Soul of Shame 42
[17] ibid pg. 44
[18] Thompson, The Soul of Shame 44

I saw a time-lapse video of the development of a baby's spine in utero, and it made me think about what a time-lapse video of my brain development would look like. I would be able to watch the development of the part of my brain that housed my fight or flight responses, then watch when the right brain and left brain start talking to each other, and later, catch a glimpse of a story being etched into the narrative part of my brain where what I believe about myself is written.

When I reached ages 12-19 of my video, I knew it would expose a lack of development in my abstract thinking, hypothetical reasoning, and planning. My personal critical thinking skills were late developing because independent thought was not taught and was discouraged in my home.

The time-lapse would help me understand that before my brain had completely developed it had processed information, stored it in my memory, and written it into my narrative. As a result, I had seen my past incorrectly and it damaged my interpersonal relationships. I now had more information, and I refined the purpose of my excavation project. I now dug to find specific events, and incomplete/incorrect information about God, Satan, and my parents. I used that information to review my memories and my narrative and was able to start rewiring my brain with truth.

There is Hope for Transformation

I was learning what it meant for my mind to flourish and I would learn how shame operated to keep that from happening as the excavation continued. As I tried to make sense of what I was learning a word picture came to mind. It helped me understand how shame had happened and how it infiltrated my mind before I began attending school.

There was an alley right beside our house. When people walked up the alley past our house they walked across our grass at the corner of the yard. It saved them a few steps, but it eventually wore a path in the grass. That was how I saw my brain. In a fully developed integrated mind, events that happened to me would have passed through all nine functions of my brain. Logical processing and consideration of the consequences, etc. would all have been in play. However, when shame was introduced repeatedly without the capacity to properly process it, the pain and shame took a shortcut straight to the narrative part of my brain. A path was worn (technically my neurons fire and neurons that fire together wire together[19]) and lies were permanently fixed in my story. The grass had been worn away.

In my word picture how could Dad have gotten rid of that path in our yard? How could he have made people stop cutting the corner and wearing a path in the grass? He could have erected a fence. That would have stopped further damage, but it wouldn't have made the grass come back. In order for that to happen Dad would have had to dig up the soil, plant new grass, and then give it time to grow before we would no longer see the scar of the path.

I had to keep doing the hard work commanded in Romans 12:1-2, "…be transformed by the renewal of your mind." (ESV). That is what writing this book was all about. It's about how I had to dig up the lies; how I found and memorized the truth that refutes the lies. But what about the fence? How could I stop the lies before they cut a new path? I had to take the first step by being vulnerable enough to share the lies. I had to learn to forgive where needed. I needed to live in community with friends and family who could help me remember who I was in Christ. I realized this was a lifelong process called sanctification.

Dr. Thompson also referenced Romans 12:1-2 when he said, "It is fair to say that although Paul was not a

---

[19] Thompson, The Soul of Shame, 47

neuroscientist, he refers here to what we now see through the lens of neuroplasticity, the ability of the brain to form and reorganize synaptic connections. Renewal of the mind, therefore, is not just an abstraction. It means real change in real bodies."[20]

It Started in the Garden

Adam and Eve had been in the garden of Eden living their best life taking care of the garden, enjoying each other's company and spending time with God. Genesis 2:25, "And the man and his wife were both naked and were not *ashamed*." (italics mine). Chapter three told me how shame actively and intentionally showed up in the garden of Eden. You can read the story for yourself in Genesis 3:1-5, but the bottom line is Satan was able to make Eve doubt God by posing the question "Did God actually say…?". When she answered him, he then told her that God had lied to her. God had said if they ate the fruit they would die. Satan said, "no you won't." I thought, *That's where shame started.* As soon as they disobeyed God's command, shame had happened. I knew this because of Genesis 3:7 "Then the eyes of them both were opened, and they knew that they were naked." They immediately sewed fig leaves together and hid from God. You don't run, hide, and cover up if you aren't ashamed. Doctor Thompson said this about Eve's encounter with Satan, "His intention is to fool the woman. And to be fooled is to be shamed, if even at the subtlest non-conscious level of awareness."[21] A final quote sheds light on the serpent's plan, "He is far more interested in disrupting the relationship between the woman, God and the man."[22]

---

[20] Thompson, Soul of Shame, 47
[21] Thompson, Soul of Shame, 100-101
[22] Ibid, 101

So What?

Lord Jesus,

Understanding, how my brain worked and how the serpent had infiltrated Eve's mind gave me the answer to one of my original questions, "That voice inside my head – where did it come from?" You showed me that Satan had disrupted Eve's mind with doubt that doubt led to questioning. Questioning led her to rewrite her narrative about who You are. Then, because she thought she was missing out and that You, God, were holding out on her, she ate of the fruit of the tree of the knowledge of good and evil. That's where the voice inside my head that lies to me came from. It came from the part of my brain where my narrative was written. It started before my brain was developed enough to be able to recognize the lie. The serpent hasn't changed his tactics. He got me to doubt and to question and to write lies into my narrative that left me covered in shame. In the New Testament book of Ephesians, you had Paul warn your church in Ephesus that they are going to need to be aware of the devil's schemes. His cunning arts, deceit, craftiness, and trickery led to the lies I believed and kept me from the truth of who You are.

What I didn't understand as I started on this journey was that at the same time Satan's lies were being written into my narrative Your truth was also being written there.

I have refreshed my memory about Your names, and this will help me be able to find You in my narrative.

Thank you, Jesus, for loving me.

Amen

CHAPTER THREE – GROUND ZERO

I am fearfully and wonderfully made.
Psalm 139:14

Knit Together

"Yes, for the 10th time, you got your girl," Dad said to Mom the morning I was born. She had been given some ether during delivery and after I was taken to the nursery, she had fallen asleep. Every time she woke up, she would ask Dad if she had gotten her girl. She asked this because she already had two boys at home. This was my ground zero. I had dug through all the decades of my life until I got back to the beginning, October 1, 1951. But was that really my ground zero?

That God was infinite and eternal were two attributes of God that amazed me the most and I was overwhelmed and ecstatic the day I read the words from Isaiah 57:15 that told me God "inhabits eternity." It was almost too much to take in. God lives in and occupies eternity. I walked around all day being overwhelmed by this truth. I shared those words, *inhabits eternity*, with everyone who would listen. God is outside of time. He knew my past, my present, and my future all at the same time. My God had chosen my parents and according to Psalm 139:16 all the days that had been formed for me were already written in God's book. My ground zero started even before the womb.

My finite brain couldn't really comprehend all of that but what I could comprehend helped me as I kept digging for and finding the lies that had been woven into my story.

Where is the Joy?

During a conversation around the dinner table one evening with my son and his family I said to the grandchildren, "I was asleep when your dad was born." The kids were speechless. What about skin-to-skin one of them asked. There had been no skin-to-skin attachment as he was born. Wayne hadn't been allowed in the room and my son, Nathan, had been whisked back to the nursery and it was several hours before I ever saw him or touched him. We had missed something very important that would have long lasting ramifications. We had not been given the opportunity for secure attachment. A Google search indicated that skin-to-skin contact at birth was crucial for establishing a bond, promoting physical and emotional well-being. As I thought about that I realized the same thing had happened when I was born.

Nathan and I both had missed out on one of the primary tasks of an infant – "acquiring a joyful, securely attached relationship"[23]

The father of lies, the devil, my shame attendant, had not stood idly by and allowed the joy and secure attachment we had both missed at birth to take place in our lives as we grew. There is another way that shame showed up early in our stories. Research suggests that shame can happen as early as fifteen to eighteen months and "usually involves a child's response to someone's nonverbal cues– a glance, tone of voice, body language, gestures, or intensity of behavior – that interrupt whatever the child may be doing, delivering a subtle but undeniably felt message of disapproval."[24]

I had heard someone say that we parent the way we were parented if we don't learn something else. My parents had

---

[23] Thompson, The Soul of Shame, 60
[24] Thompson, Soul of Shame, 62

done better than their parents, but my siblings and I had regularly been the recipients of the glances, tone of voice, body language, gestures, and intensity of behavior that delivered those subtle messages of disapproval. This continued for my son as well.

One example of how shame showed up in body language for me came from a picture of Dad and me. It had been my favorite picture of us and had been sitting in a frame in my bedroom. I retrieved the picture and looked at it again. I was about two years old; it was summertime and Dad's 1950 Chrysler was parked in the grass at a campground. Dad and I were stooped down beside the car. He was wearing jeans and a t-shirt, and I was wearing a little summer dress. I loved that picture. In my mind's eye when I remembered it Dad's arm was around me. It made me feel loved as Daddy's little girl. I was shocked when I realized that Dad wasn't touching me - I was touching him. My little hand rested on his leg, but his arms were folded across his legs. There was no evidence of any emotional connection between us. It hurt my heart. The voice inside my head (my shame attendant) said, "See, your dad didn't really love you." Was that true?

The next time I visited Dawn I took the picture of Dad and me by the car. As we started the session I said, "My father was full-blood Dutch, born in 1910." She replied, "That's all I need to know." It wasn't all I needed to know. God was going to use the genealogy I had found in the attic to gently brush away the lie that Dad didn't love me and many other lies as well.

Coming to America

Stubborn is the first word that comes to mind when I think about my Dutch heritage. My mother described what being Dutch meant for my dad. She said, "Albert not only sets his foot, but he also braces it." Once he made up his mind there was no changing it. I uncovered articles telling about how my grandmother's family had immigrated from Holland to America in 1847. I also learned that my grandfather's family came in 1849. My dad's grandfather was the first one in his family that was born in America. Why was that information important? It was important because Dad was only the third generation born in America after his family had left Holland as a result of religious persecution. I wondered if I would be able to find an answer to why my dad and his family were emotionally distant if I could learn the whole story of them coming to America. Any emotional baggage that had come with them would still have been affecting my dad as a child.

Running on Empty,[25] by Dr. Jonice Webb, a book I read as I researched my parent's lives, talked about what the author called emotional neglect. The first time I heard that word I bristled, "My parents did not neglect me." Neglect in my mind was intentional, and I did not believe that my parents had intentionally neglected me, but the true definition of neglect is *failure to give proper attention.*[26] That definition made sense, and it was true. I wanted to know why Dad had not given proper attention to my emotions.

I researched the history of the persecution my ancestors had experienced and found that it had been going on for a long time before the first group of immigrants boarded ships to come to America. Why did that matter? Because that's where the emotional neglect quite possibly started.

It Didn't Start with Me

The people who had been influential in Dad's parents' lives were hardworking, committed, and brave. One of Dad's

---

[25] Dr. Jonice Webb, Running on Empty (New York, Morgan James Publishing, 2014)

[26] https://www.oed.com/search/dictionary/?scope=Entries&q=neglect

relatives was in that first group of immigrants. I'm going to let her tell you the story.

It had taken over ten years for us to get to that day[27]. The persecution really started back in 1816 when King Willima I got involved in religious issues and made rules for the Government of the Reformed Church. Those rules had been approved by Royal Decree and from then on things got worse and worse. As the state-supported clergy gradually assumed great power the church became an institution of form and not faith. As a result, our group seceded from the Dutch Reformed Church. We believed in the complete separation of church and state. Pastor Hendrik Scholte became our leader. He had been suspended from the Dutch Reformed Church.

Our group became known as the dissenters, and we were denied the right to assemble in groups of more than 19 people. We held our services in homes, barns, and even under hay sheds. There were also times when we just met out under the open sky. That was a very difficult and scary time for us. Every time we met we wondered if the soldiers would show up. And they did. One day while Pastor Scholte was preaching from a farmer's cart, soldiers came and ordered us to disperse. We refused and the soldiers cut that cart into splinters with Pastor still on it. He went down with the wreck; he was arrested and was imprisoned for three weeks.

That sparked the discussions that led to the decision for us to leave our beloved homeland. That's how we found ourselves in April of 1847, on the dock in Rotterdam, Holland. We were ready to load the four ships that had been sitting there in the harbor waiting for us. There were 800 of us. The majority of us had come from the well-to-do agricultural class and had owned our own farms. We had

---

[27] https://www.pellahistorical.org/historyofpella

agreed to receive as members of the new colony only sober, industrious, moral persons.

It had been very hard to get packed. We had to decide what to take and what to leave behind knowing that we would never see it again. I made sure that all my photographs were included in what I packed. I remember the pain I felt when I hugged, for the last time, those I was leaving behind. There was no relief from the fear, the pain, and the grief when we finally boarded those ships.

When we boarded, we discovered the ships were disgustingly filthy. Once we set sail, we didn't complain. Everyone got to work and cleaned those ships from top to bottom. Every day when we weren't cleaning, we were meeting for worship services. The captains said that they had never brought more orderly or better-behaved people across the Atlantic.

In my imaginary conversation with Great-Great-Great Grandma I stopped her and told her a little story. I said, "That story about how you cleaned the ship reminded me of a story my mom told me. Your great granddaughter, Nellie, became my mom's mother-in- law. They were on their hand and knees scrubbing the floor at grandma's house one day when my mom leaned back, wiped her forehead, and said, 'This is hard work.' Grandma replied, 'And hard work ain't easy.' I think she was saying, – quit your whining and scrub." Let's get back to your story.

It had been a very hard trip. The fastest ship arrived in Baltimore in 26 days, and it had taken the last one 60 days. We added more grief during the trip as a few of our group died. The journey wasn't over. We unloaded the ships and then reloaded everything onto the trains that took us to Columbia, Pennsylvania. We were all exhausted and anxious about the next leg of our trip. We boarded canal boats that took us to Pittsburgh, Pennsylvania. From there we travelled down the Ohio River to St. Louis. We stayed in St Louis for a few weeks. A committee had been chosen and they travelled west, found and purchased land. While they were gone, we experienced more grief as we lost many more of our group due to the extreme heat. When the committee returned and told us of their purchase, there was a rare time of rejoicing.

In August of 1847, four months from the time we left our homes, farms, and communities in Holland, we arrived physically and emotionally tired at the place that had been named Pella, Iowa. Pella in Hebrew meant 'city of refuge.' Our city of refuge didn't have any houses, or farms, or schools yet. It was just part of the prairie. Most of us spent our first winter in dugouts with roofs made of straw.

The next years as we built our homes, businesses, schools, and church continued to be difficult. It had been hard, hard work. In 1861 the Civil war started and over 100 of our young men went to fight. Twenty-four did not return[28]. These are my memories of that time."

Dad's ancestors spent years living in fear before they ever left Holland. The continued fear and grief as well as the fatigue of travel made it safe to say that they had been running on empty and had brought with them a great deal of emotional baggage. Not having the ability or the resources to unpack that emotional baggage would have created some generational trauma for my dad's family. According to the Google definition, generational trauma occurs when a group of people experience a significant and deeply distressing event. The trauma is then passed down through generations, affecting the children, grandchildren, and even great grandchildren of the original survivors.

---

[28] https://www.pellahistorical.org/

So What?

Heavenly Father,

I agree with what Pastor Spence said in his sermon from the ten commandments. "…Parents have a powerful presence in our lives. There is NO QUESTION, the greatest influencers on how we function as adults are the people who raised us. They are certainly not the only influencer, but they are the greatest. The language you speak is determined by who raises you, what you value, the assumptions you have about the way the world works, even your beliefs about God are all massively influenced by the people who raised you. How you respond to situations and circumstances…your very instincts were shaped through watching your parents. The emotional baggage we carry with us…a lot of us got that from our relationship with our parents."[29]

You will use the information I have learned about how Satan uses my brain to get me to doubt You, to help me as I start unpacking my emotional baggage. As I think about your name, Jehovah-Jireh – The Lord Will Provide, I think about all the information you have provided to me in the storage boxes from the attic; information that will dispel lies and expose truth.

Thank you.

Amen

---

[29] https://mercycharlotte.com/sermons/the-fifth-commandment-the-power-of-our-parents/

CHAPTER FOUR – MEET THE PARENTS

"The Lord is gracious and merciful, …abounding in steadfast love."
Psalm 145:8-9

As I worked through the genealogy doing some more calculating I learned about some new trauma in Dad's life that would definitely become baggage he carried into fatherhood. My dad died in 1986 so I couldn't ask him any questions but using the information I collected from my research I could let him tell the first part of the story.

Deep Sadness for Dad

"It was Tuesday, October 29, 1918, my mom and dad Frank (34) and Nellie (28) Van Gorp who had been married for twelve years, welcomed baby David to our family. They had moved from Pella to New Sharon. They already had five children, the oldest was ten and the youngest was two. 1918 was the year the Spanish flu pandemic swept across the world killing millions and it stopped at our house.

Wednesday, October 30th the flu took my ten-year-old sister Elizabeth. On Thursday, October 31st, Richard, my four-year-old brother I called Dickey, also lost his life to the flu.

Saturday, November 1st baby David only four days old died. And then on Tuesday, November 5th two-year-old Everette did not survive the flu.

38

My Mom also had the flu. She was so sick that she did not know her children had died until after she got well. In just one week our family of eight became a family of four.

My name is Albert. I am eight years old. My seven-year-old sister, Mattie, and I are the two children who survived."

To think about how much grief Dad had experienced in such a short time broke my heart. I tried to go there with him in my mind. I saw him - probably in worn overalls, maybe barefoot, with tousled red hair. He lost his big sister, who had been his playmate and chore partner. He had been big brother to Dickey and Everette. I wondered if he had even gotten to hold baby David. So much tragedy in such a short time. That had to have done something to Dad's heart. It would have done something to his brain, too. What I learned about how the brain works let me know that his fight or flight instinct would have engaged. He would have perceived the loss of his family as a threat to his own survival.

His parents and grandparents were his influencers during that time. He would have taken his cues from them about dealing with grief. In the fact-based novel that his mom's cousin wrote, she described his ancestors as self-contained and un-demonstrative. With the amount of grief and loss he and his ancestors had experienced that description made sense.

Dad was thirteen when his family left Iowa and moved to Indiana. There was more to learn about Dad's formative years that was going to help me understand him so much better. He continues his story.

More Hard Things

I had been enrolled in school after we moved but, because my dad didn't value education, I dropped out and went to work with him doing construction.

I was nineteen the day the stock market crashed on October 24, 1929. It was a very bad day for the country and for my family as well. One evening not long after that, there was a knock at the door during dinner. My dad answered the door, returned to the table, picked up his water glass, and threw it at the wall. The visitor had informed him that the bank that held his construction loans had failed. His five construction projects were gone. My family was quickly in crisis. That night changed everyone's life. I went back to Iowa and worked on a farm for $30.00 a month and sent the money back to my family so they could put food on their table. Mattie was seventeen, Leonard was nine and Edna was only four. I became their provider and protector, a role I would continue to play for the rest of my life.

I moved back to Indiana and had several jobs as the depression continued for ten years. I owned a 1932 Buick four door sedan and worked at the lead foundry. It was April of 1937 when I got home late one night and found my dad waiting to talk to me about the Lord. The next day I went to church, talked to the pastor, and surrendered my life to Christ. The Sunday night I walked down the aisle at church to make my profession public, I didn't know there was a young lady named, Louise Melton in the congregation. She saw me when I walked past her. She later told me, "It was as clear as if the person sitting next to me said, 'There goes your husband.'" Louise heard right, I became her husband and together we became the great influencers in your life.

Mom's Timeline

Now that I knew about Dad, I wanted to learn more about Mom too. I didn't find as much of my Mom's history as I had my Dad's. Mom died in 1995 so I couldn't ask any more questions. I did have Mom's little slips of paper and 3x5 cards that contained her hand written genealogy. I found them after she died. She didn't have the technology to build a spreadsheet, but I did. She left birth, death, and wedding dates for her and all of her siblings. She had also left handwritten stories about how her mom and dad met. This is one of them.

The Terrell family and the Melton family lived in Christian County, Ky in the late 1800s. (How everyone got to Christian County, Kentucky to begin with will forever be a mystery.) *The Melton's had five boys and five girls. The Terrell family had four boys and two girls. Both families moved to Indiana where they met, and the seven girls became friends.*

One day when the Terrell girls were visiting the Melton girls, Henry, one of the Melton boys came in the kitchen and said to his sister, "Who is that little fat girl with the window in her teeth?" The sister replied, "That's Nannie Terrell." Henry said, "Well, she's going to be my wife." He was right, Henry Melton (21) and Nannie Terrell (21) were married December 23, 1908.

Over the next thirteen years they would have seven children.

Talking To Mom

"Mom, I looked at some of the dates in your genealogy and I saw that just like Dad you had experienced the death of siblings. You weren't quite five when Ralph died and you were six and a half when Daniel died; old enough to remember, I'm sure. In your first twelve years of life, you experienced the birth of three sisters and three brothers. You also experienced the death of two of those brothers. Being the oldest it became your responsibility to take care of the new baby. As you both grew up you were often mistaken as Edna's mother and not her sister. She described you as her "second mother," her counselor and her friend.

From the stories you told I learned that while your dad was a hard worker, he wasn't always a very nice man. He had been spoiled by his sisters and was rather narcissistic. That assumption is based on the stories you told about how your mom had to have his work clothes starched and ironed so he could strut down the street to work. He was a brakeman on the railroad so that starch and press wouldn't have lasted long once he got to work.

He was a very authoritarian parent and according to Dr Webb, "Authoritarian parents require a lot from their children. The children are expected to follow their parents' rules without questioning them. At the same time, these parents don't explain the reasons behind their rules. They simply require adherence and crack down harshly when the child doesn't comply. They are not particularly concerned with the feelings or ideas of the child."[30]

Life in Mom's House

This story about an interaction Mom had with her dad is an example of the authoritarian parenting style. She tells; *I was in the bedroom with my sisters one night when Dad called for us to come to the living room. We said, "in a minute." He replied, "If I had wanted you in a minute I would have waited until in a minute to call you." From then on, "coming" was our response.*

More of her story clearly shows the family dynamic. *At supper one night Dad cut open his hot biscuit, then used that knife to cut his butter. The butter slides off his hot knife onto the table. He tried to scoop it up, but it kept falling off. In frustration he used his knife and smeared the butter all over the table. My mom couldn't leave it alone. She said, "Now don't you feel really proud of yourself?"*

---

[30] Dr Jonice Webb, Running on Empty, pg. 19

When I was a senior in high school, I only owned two dresses, one for weekdays and one for Sunday. They were a size 44. I weighed 225 pounds and was only 5' 4" tall.

I had been a good student and loved to learn. Because I had been lefthanded, I had been made to stay after school and learn to write with my right hand. After all that hard work I was very proud when a few years later I won the penmanship award. After I completed one semester of college, I wasn't able to continue because my dad hadn't paid the bill. It was then that my sister, Helen, and I left home and went to live in northern Indiana with an aunt. We worked together in a pie bakery when we first arrived. I never forgot how to bake a wonderful pie.

After the pie bakery I worked at the department store behind the candy counter. Employees were allowed to eat as much candy as they wanted. My favorite snack was Spanish peanuts. My next job was as a live-in nanny for my doctor. All those Spanish peanuts led to gallbladder problems but because I was so heavy he couldn't do surgery. The doctor put me on a very strict diet. I was allowed a poached egg on toast and a cup of tea three times a day until I lost enough weight to have the surgery. I never gained it all back, but I was still heavy enough that I had self-image problems.

The only part of Mom's faith journey that I knew about was that she had given her life to Christ when she was nine years old and she started praying for her husband at the same time. She and her three sisters all played the piano and sang together. After she moved north, she found a church and became the church pianist. She had never been on a date, had a boyfriend or been kissed when the man she had spent twenty years praying for walked down the aisle that Sunday in April of 1937.

Faith and the Culture

The late 1920's had seen foundational disputes in many churches about the role of Christianity; the authority of the Bible; and the death, resurrection, and atoning sacrifice of Jesus Christ. This became known as the fundamentalist-modernist controversy.[31] The church where my parents met was a fundamentalist church and was a member of the Independent Fundamental Churches of America. Much like how the change in the church led to my dad's family leaving Holland, the changes in the church in America led to the fundamentalist movement.

Prohibition hadn't stopped the flow of alcohol. It just led to bootlegging and the speakeasy culture. Hollywood's contribution to the first half of the era included movies depicting gangsters, prostitutes, sleazy backroom politicians, and lawyers. Even the comedy of the Marx Brothers, W.C. Field and May West expressed disdain for traditional institutions and values.

Just as my parent's personal biblical beliefs had not mirrored the modernist view, their personal convictions had not mirrored what was going on in society. As I researched this information, I better understood how their convictions emerged. Merriam-Webster defined a conviction as "a strong persuasion or belief."[32]

Those convictions that included not going to the movies, not drinking or frequenting places that served alcohol, or dancing or smoking made perfect sense to them. Their convictions had come from their love for the Lord and their desire to be obedient to what they believed God's Word taught. For example, this verse from I Thessalonians 5:22

---

[31]

https://en.wikipedia.org/wiki/Fundamentalist%E2%80%93modernist_controversy
[32] https://www.merriam-webster.com/dictionary/conviction

44

"Abstain from every form of evil," I needed to talk to Mom about some things.

The Two Became One

Dear Mom,

I don't know how you would have felt about us finding and reading your diary, but I'm so glad we did. We got to watch you two crazy kids fall in love. The first entry you made on January 1, 1938, says, "Have been going with Albert since December 4th." Eight months after you first laid eyes on him, you were dating.

It is so sweet to read your love story; to see a side of both of you through a different lens that isn't clouded with lies. From the pages of your diary, I learned about your good friends, Roy and Elsie, and that you had lots of fun together. I had no idea that Dad had ever held a fishing pole, yet I learned it was a favorite activity for Dad and Roy.

I could feel that giddy falling in love excitement you had as you wrote, "Just think of it. I'm the first girl he ever loved and tho' he doesn't know why; he loves me more than he can ever tell me. How do I know? Because he told me so and I believe him. He's the grandest fellow I know anywhere." Never having seen or experienced much affection from Dad, it was good to read this entry written shortly before you got engaged. You also wrote that Dad said, "I could squeeze the life out of you. The only time I'm content is when I'm with you, Honey."

There is one entry that made me incredibly sad as it showed how you too had been infected with shame. You wrote about how proud you were when you took Dad to meet your parents. "I was so proud of him I could have strutted all over town. I do not know why he loves an old cow like me, but he <u>does</u>." My heart hurt for you because I could relate to those *feelings of body shame. When I looked at the pictures of you from that time, I saw that I got your body shape. And even though you were overweight it sure didn't look like it bothered Dad.*

Reading your diary confirmed my belief that the provider/protector part of Dad had consumed his life before he met you. I saw that he started to learn what it meant to have fun when he began to interact with your family. Your family had its own issues, but they did know how to have fun. This was the entry that told about the trip you took to southern Indiana so Dad could meet your parents and you could get your marriage license, "Albert had a grand time he thinks my folks are swell, and so do I. He had the grandest time he ever had in his life," you wrote. If the fishing, fried chicken dinner with all the trimmings, ice cream and cake and hanging out with your family constituted the "grandest time of his life" the self-contained and non-demonstrative title had been accurate.

March 19, 1938, the night Dad proposed, you wrote, "He's really the most wonderful person in all the world and I vow to spend the rest of my life just making him happy. I thank God for him and earnestly pray that he may never be sorry he asked me to be his wife." It was August of 1938 when after praying for him for twenty years you married him. You looked so happy in your wedding pictures. You were proud of the white leather shoes you had found on the sale rack and cleaned up. Your friends, Roy and Elsie were on hand to be your attendants.

In the fall of 1942, three years after you got married, you moved to New York and both of you attended Practical Bible Training School in Binghamton. Dad worked as the night watchman at the school and was able to study while he worked. You both graduated with a diploma in

Bible/Theology after completing the three-year program in 30 months.

One of the treasures I found in my stash was the page from the 1944 yearbook that had both of your pictures and life verses. Dad's verse was I Corinthians 15:58 (KJV), "Therefore, my beloved brethren, be ye steadfast, unmoveable, always abounding in the work of the Lord, forasmuch as ye know that your labour is not in vain in the Lord." He lived that verse. It was one of the verses I had in my memory bank because I had heard it quoted so many times growing up.

Mom, your verse reflected you as well. Psalm 16:8 (KJV), "I have set the Lord always before me: because he is at my right hand, I shall not be moved." And you weren't ever moved that I saw. Regardless of what life threw at you, you stayed steadfast in your faith.

Their Next Step

Armed with their education, their life verses, their love for each other and God, they moved to Michigan after graduation. They were part of a mission that would find a community with a church building that had been closed and reopen it. They stayed friends with one of the families for many years after they left. I remember when we made a trip back there so Dad could perform the wedding ceremony for one of the daughters.

July 10, 1947, Phil was born. They both were thirty-six years old and had been married for nine years. Dad had been going to Indiana during the week to work with his dad and would go back to Michigan on the weekends. I found the letter you wrote to him on your ninth wedding anniversary.

My Dear Honey,

Just sitting here thinking of the nice evening we spent together nine years ago tonight. I remember how happy we both were to think that was the last night we'd say good night, and you'd go away. Little did we know how wrong we were. We couldn't know that after nine years we'd have to be separated even on our anniversary. I also remember the night we decided we wanted a family, but we wanted to wait for a year. Little did we know we'd wait almost nine years.

Since you aren't here tonight, I just had to let you know how much you mean to me. The example of your life has meant a lot to me. I've learned many lessons in Christian living and tho' I fall far short of what I'd like to be I'm a better Christian because of you. ...Our love has grown and ripened thro' the years, we have an understanding of each other which we didn't have nine years ago, and we now have our precious little Philip to make our home complete.

Complete? Who said it's complete? Sixteen months later, in November of 1948, Tim was born. I'm not sure what year it was when Mom and the boys moved to Indiana too. They lived with Grandma and Grandpa for a while before they were able to rent their own place. Dad had become the bi-vocational pastor of a small congregation that met in the administration building of a housing project. He was still doing construction work with his dad. Some of those construction projects included a house for Mom and Dad, one for Mom's brother Hank, one for Dad's brother Leonard and one for his sister, Edna.

Their Next Adventure Begins

The housing project where the church met was named Columbia Center. It had been built in 1941 and housed 400 families in two square blocks. The tenants were low income and had been living in substandard housing prior to moving to the Center. Because their income level didn't qualify them to live in the Center, their new house had been built across the street on the east side.

However, it wasn't yet time for Dad to put his tools away. The church congregation had outgrown the administration building they used for church. Property had been purchased as close as possible to the Center on the west side. Because of his construction background he became the general contractor and did much of the finish carpentry work along with his dad.

From everything I learned about my parent's families and experiencing life as their daughter, I knew that they both had been raised in an authoritarian environment with parents who were running on empty. Dr Webb said, "One of the unfortunate aspects of Emotional Neglect is that it's self-propagating. Emotionally neglected children grow up with a blind spot about emotions, their own as well as those of others."[33]

Dr Webb had listed twelve different styles of parenting that led to Emotional Neglect. For example: Narcissistic, Authoritarian, Permissive, Addicted, and Depressed. Even though the Authoritarian style fit them she had one that fit even better. She called it "The Well-Meaning-but-Neglected-Themselves-Parent. It is possible for a parent who loves and wants the best for their children to emotionally neglect them. They loved their children, but authoritarian parenting was all that they knew.

Dear Dawn,

During one of our sessions, you taught me something that reshaped how I viewed my parents emotional neglect as well as all the other events that had deeply wounded me. You told me that in order to re-story my life I needed to construct new meaning from old narratives; I had to start with

---

[33]Jonice Webb, *Running on Empty* (New York: Morgan James Publishing,2014) 67

understanding that God was sovereign. I had to remember that He had always been in control and that He had known my story from eternity past. I had to know that Satan, my shame attendant, always meant evil but God brought good; that when I was able to break the silence about my wounds and heartbreak they would no longer have center stage in my story. The events had happened, but they could now be moved to the background. Let the restory begin.

Gratefully, Rachel

So What?

Lord Jesus,

Your name, Elohim, shows up in the first verse of the Bible. "In the beginning, God, [Elohim] created the earth. And you never stopped creating.

Isaiah 43: 1,3-4, 7 says, … "I am the LORD your God [*Elohim*] …you are precious in My sight…. Everyone who is called by My name, and **whom I have created for My glory**, (bold mine) whom I have formed, even whom I have made."

I know from reading the Bible that family heritage is important to you. There are genealogies all through scripture. The stories of Abraham, Isaac, Jacob, and Joseph, to name a few, tell me about their parents and give me details of their lives that help me know and understand them better. None of their parents were perfect but that didn't stop you from using them and their children.

My genealogy is important too. There wouldn't be a Rachel if there hadn't been an Albert and Louise. You chose my parents. You knew what they had and didn't have to give. I am exactly as you, Elohim, designed me to be. And that design has a purpose – to bring you glory.

Something happened as I understood more about Mom and Dad. I began to feel compassion for them. I have also been able to confess and repent of my bitterness and resentment toward them. Both of those things have been healing. I have a new perspective as I start to excavate the first years of my life.

Amen

CHAPTER FIVE – LITTLE RACHEL SPEAKS

"Shame can't survive being spoken. Shame needs three things to survive: secrecy, silence, and judgement." Brené Brown

Pictures Told the Story

Like hieroglyphics on a caveman's wall some of the pictures I retrieved from the attic uncovered information about the first three years of my life. I found one of me on a blanket propped up in the corner of the couch for my first photo shoot. There I was as a toddler looking content in two of the pictures as I enjoyed being outside in the playpen. I love the one where I posed on the back porch with six little boys clutching my pail and shovel just waiting to get back to playing in the dirt. The pail and shovel showed up in several pictures as I dug in the dirt of what had yet to become a landscaped yard.

My Baby Book was one of the treasures from the attic. Mom wrote about a conversation I had with my brother. Tim called her a baby. "I not, I two now," she replied.

I had claimed the neighbor's row of flowers that was between our two houses as my own. The first time I saw snow on them I declared, "It rained a puddle on my flowers." The time it had taken her to make those entries in the baby book deconstructed the lies that Mom had been too busy to care; a belief I carried about my mom for many years.

And Then There Were Four

My earliest memory is shortly after I had my third birthday. I was kneeling on the sofa and watching out the front room window as I waited excitedly for Dad to bring Mom and my new baby sister, Ruth, home from the hospital. Dad and Mom were forty-four, Phil was seven, and Tim was six. Ruth's arrival completed our family. Ruth had a head full of red corkscrew curls that drew everyone's attention. I always felt like I was on the outside looking in when all the attention was on Ruth. Being the third child and oldest daughter played a big role in how I viewed myself and led to some of my "not good enough" feelings. I would realize years later that Ruth had gotten attention just by "being." I tried to get attention by "doing."

Good Behavior Expected

Fast forward a few months to Sunday mornings, and our lives as the four preacher's kids in a rules-based church with no nursery.

It's divide and conquer time for Mom and Dad. Mom is at the piano in charge of the girls. Dad is on the platform and is in charge of the boys. Ruth, in her baby seat, was on the floor beside Mom. I was in a highchair on the other side. Phil and Tim, who are six and seven, were on the front row where Dad could see them. This is how it was every Sunday.

I remember hearing about one specific Sunday when the boys started to misbehave. The boys were dressed in jeans and t-shirts. Mom didn't want anyone to think they had to have "Sunday Best" clothes to come to church. Phil and Tim started picking at each other. All of a sudden, my dad paused right in the middle of a sentence, looked at the congregation, then at my brothers and said, "Excuse me folks, I have a discipline problem to take care of." He left the platform, gave each boy a swat, and returned to the sermon.

Authoritarian parenting style in action! The boys had been expected to behave and the punishment for misbehavior had been given quickly and without regard to their feelings. I also believe that the fear of what people would think about the preacher's kids misbehaving was a factor in his decision to discipline so publicly. He thought he was setting a good example for his congregation. I'm sure Mom was very embarrassed.

I asked my brother about the incident, and he didn't remember it. He did, however, remember the time Dad spanked him because he called one of the ladies a fat cow. Dad told him he hadn't been spanked because the statement wasn't true, he was spanked because he said it.

This wasn't the only traumatic moment for me as a church kid... one of the hardest events – one I would need to process for years to come, happened when I was four years old.

Trauma Enters

Dear Mom,

You never knew what happened to me when I was four years old. One Sunday morning I needed to use the restroom and went downstairs by myself. I went down the two short flights of stairs into the fellowship hall and walked past the Sunday school classrooms that were on my right. I turned down the little hallway where the restrooms were. As I was walking back to the steps something awful happened. Mr. Davies, the old man who came to our church, was standing there and he looked very scary. He took me into the children's Sunday school room that had the shorter tables. My heart was pounding very hard, and I didn't like what was happening when he got me to stand on top of the table. I wondered why he would want me to stand on the table. I knew that wasn't right. The next thing he did was so horrible I never told you or anyone else about it. He put his hand in my panties. It was frightening, and I started to cry. He took his hand out and I got down from the table as fast as I could and ran back upstairs.

I was in my thirties when I finally told Wayne. He had come up behind me when I was at the kitchen sink and touched me in a way that triggered the memory. I didn't know why it had taken me so long to tell anyone about it. When I talked to Dawn about it at one of our sessions, she explained it like this. "Cognitively you had no frame of reference to make sense of this event. Your body, however, registered shame and the belief that you were bad was written deeply into your narrative."

Several years before I talked to Dawn I had discussed the trauma with a different counselor. He had explained another part of the harm. He told me, "The harm was personal, it was unfair, and it was deep. It damaged your ability to trust. In your four-year-old mind you determined that it wasn't safe to trust anyone, and you locked up emotionally." It wouldn't be the last time I experienced hurt, but it set a precedent for how I would deal with hurt in the future. I lived my life trying to protect myself. The shame attendant added the shame from this trauma to my already emotionally neglected heart.

Sadly, Rachel

The molestation had been another way that evil had stolen my joy. Over the years when this memory would surface, I would think to myself, *It was no big deal, it only happened one time. Many people have had it a lot worse.* However, that "only one time" and the shame that had accompanied it had been firmly planted in my brain. Life went on and I continued to grow physically, mentally, spiritually, and socially. It would be many years before I understood how deeply that event had damaged my emotions.

Any time I read or heard about children that had been victimized, I wondered why God allowed those things to happen. As I worked on this chapter, I read a blog post that gave me some clarity. The author, Scotty Smith, a pastor in Franklin, Tennessee had written, "Lord Jesus, we'll never experience a wounding greater than the promise of your healing. None of our traumas in life – and the combined impact of them all, happen outside the domain of your knowing, ruling, and caring. That is both comforting and confusing. But it's way more comforting than the thought of living life in a world in which happenstance has more control and power than providence."

He continued, "Nothing would be ***more traumatic*** than to think of you passively watching us from afar – unmoved and powerless to do anything about our losses, betrayals, abuses, and harmings. You are ***near*** the broken-hearted – you don't promise we won't get our hearts broken and our spirits crushed in our journey Home. Jesus, I'd rather have your nearness than a life of never getting hurt. I'd rather live in the paradox of Joseph's words to his brother – "What you meant for evil, God meant for good" (Gen 50:20) – than to think evil is more sovereign than you – the eternal King of heaven and earth."[34]

So What?

Lord Jesus,

I've learned that shame can't survive being spoken. When I was able to expose what had been kept secret, speak what had not been shared, and call out the shame attendant the re-storying process was started.

The Bible doesn't condone everything that it records. We can clearly see that evil happens. No one can be more sovereign than You because two sovereigns are an oxymoron. Sovereignty is the attribute by which You rule Your entire

---

[34] https://www.thegospelcoalition.org/blogs/scotty-smith/be-done-with-minimizing-weaponizing-and-pretending/

creation. To be sovereign You must be all-knowing, all-powerful, and absolutely free. I learned from A. W. Tozer[35] that if there were even one datum of knowledge, however small, that was unknown to You, Your rule would break down at that point. Lord Jesus, You possess all knowledge. If You were lacking even one infinitesimal modicum of power, that lack would end Your reign and undo Your kingdom; that one stray atom of power would belong to someone else, and You would be a limited ruler and then not sovereign.

Your name that represents this attribute is, El Elyon: God Most High. I read in Kay Arthur's book, *To Know Him By Name*[36] that if You are not sovereign, if You are not in control, if all things are not under Your dominion, then You are *not* the Most High, and I am either in the hands of blind fate, in the hands of man, or in the hands of the devil.

There is another one of Your names that is helpful especially as I process the trauma of the molestation. That name is El Roi: The God Who Sees. This won't be the only time that this name is important. This attribute represents Your Omnipresence. You never lost sight of me for one minute. You cried with me when evil hurt me. You saw the sin that was committed against me. Someday You will vindicate me because You say in Romans 12:19 "'Vengeance is mine, I will repay,' says the Lord." And that is why I can forgive Mr. Davies. I don't know if Mr. Davies ever confessed his sin and received forgiveness, only You know that. What I do know is that if he didn't there will be a day of judgement for him.

I don't know how it all works but You knew it would be hard for me to wrap my finite brain around this concept, so You explained it a bit for me in Romans 8:28 when You had

---

[35] Tozer, The Knowledge of the Holy, pg.108
[36] Kay Arthur, To Know Him by Name (Sisters Oregon: Multnomah Press, 1995) pg. 26

Paul write, "all things work together for the good of those who love You…" So, I will keep trusting You and keep excavating to find the lies and the truth that refutes the lies and I will keep finding what You promised – Healing.

Thank You for loving me and seeing me always.

Amen

CHAPTER SIX – I HAVE TO BE PERFECT & OTHER NONSENSE

*To be human is to be infected with this phenomenon
we call shame.*
Dr. Curt Thompson

Rachel Goes to School

Kids are the best recorders of events, but the worst interpreters. Many of the things I had "caught" and "recorded" in my young life I had not been cognitively able to interpret correctly. The narrative part of my brain had written my story with incomplete and incorrect information and that story was covered in shame.

I was compliant by nature and that made it easy for my shame attendant to lie to me. My parents' authoritarian parenting style was full of rules. They valued and expected compliance. The 1950's was an era when children were to be seen and not heard, and that was very true in our house. I had not been allowed to question my parents' authority. I hadn't ever questioned the rules out loud; I had just done my best to obey them. That environment allowed the lie that I needed to be perfect to take root. Not only was obedience expected but I believed that obeying the rules perfectly was what it meant to be a good Christian. I really, really wanted to be a good Christian. The lie had grown, and I needed to be perfect not only to please my parents but also, so I believed, to please God.

I Have to be Perfect

The first seven years of my life my dad was not a part of my everyday life. All of his time was taken up building churches and pastoring people. There wasn't time to be a hands-on dad when there was a church to build, sermons to prepare, hospital visits to be made and members to visit. By the time the church building had been completed I was in second grade and had no relationship with my dad. Even without the hands-on relationship I had been learning from him. He had been teaching me about what he believed to be true about God.

He showed me that he believed God's Word was important because every morning, I saw him in the kitchen with his cup of coffee and his Bible. He taught me that others were important by the way he ministered to them. He taught me that obedience was important by the way he disciplined me and my siblings.

Mom was also teaching when every morning, after my dad left, I would find my mom sitting on the couch with her Bible. I "caught" that reading my Bible was important, and that I "should" do it, too. They were setting a good example about the importance of spending time in God's Word. However, without any explanation or encouragement that helped me understand the why and the how I had been left with shame and guilt because I didn't read my Bible. When I would say, "Mom, I'm bored," the reply would be, "Go read your Bible." I had known there was a reason I *should* read my Bible and even though I hadn't known what it was, my narrative said because I didn't read my Bible, I was *wrong*. If I was wrong, then I was bad and I felt shame.

In his book *I Have to Be Perfect (and other Parsonage Heresies),*[37] Timothy Sanford explains that with the *should* thinking, I had only two options: The *should* way or the wrong way. This applied not only on the major issues of Scripture where there was a genuine right or wrong, but it got generalized into every part of my life. That either/or mindset was the catalyst for anxiety. As I had continued to believe and live the lie that I needed to be perfect, anxiety had begun to show up in many areas of my life. I hadn't understood that all of my fears came from believing I needed to be perfect. "Perfectionistic thinking is not solely based upon how perfect you want things to be, but on how you think they *should* be. Perfectionism is, in part, deep-seated thinking patterns that hold onto a concise, ridged view of how things *should* be done in order to be done *right.*"[38] I feared being wrong. I feared failing – therefore I didn't try. I also had learned to be afraid of what others thought about me. That fear in the form of "they are going to think…" ruled my whole life. I was afraid of rejection and afraid of not knowing something. Most of all, I was afraid of disappointing God, afraid because deep down I believed I needed to be perfect.

Learning Truth

In my pre-teen years, as I grew mentally and physically, I had been learning truth, and I had been growing spiritually but I didn't realize it. We didn't have television in our home, but we did have radio. *The Listening Post* was aired every weekday afternoon as Ruth and I got home from school. We got a snack, sat at the kitchen table, and listened as a chapter from one of the *"The Sugar Creek Gang"* books was read. Dragonfly, Little Jim, Circus, and their friends had always

---

[37] Timothy L. Sanford, I Have to Be Perfect (And Other Parsonage Heresies) (Colorado Springs, CO) Llama Press, 1998) 36-37
[38] Ibid pg. 97

been involved in some exciting adventure and we had been right there with them.

Sailor Sam came on next. We joined him and his friends when they set sail on Sam's schooner, *The Porpoise*. We went with them on high sea adventures exploring God's creation. Those programs taught me about kindness, respect, teamwork, and faith in God. On Saturday mornings we knew that we had chores to do. We had to clean our room, dust the living room, and help with anything else Mom asked us to do. But chores waited until *The Children's Bible Hour* and *Ranger Bill* were done. (Fun fact – I can still sing most of the words to most of the theme songs from these programs. Of course, I don't remember what I had for breakfast yesterday, but I can belt out "Raaangerrr Bill, warrior of the woodland…")

Children's Bible Hour was my favorite. Every week, Ruth and I sat on the floor in the living room and listened as Aunt Bertha and Uncle Charlie interacted with the kids in the studio audience. I loved listening to them sing and have Bible knowledge contests between the boys and the girls. I wondered if there was going be a question for the listeners to answer. If you knew the answer, you wrote to Aunt Bertha, and she would send you a prize. Many times, I sent my answer to "Aunt Bertha, Box 1, Grand Rapids, Michigan." Then I watched for the mailman every day until my prize arrived.

After the singing and the contests, it was story time. March 19, 1960, a story touched my heart, and I found Mom and told her, "I want to ask Jesus into my heart." She took me into her bedroom and we knelt on the rug beside her bed. With her help I prayed and told Jesus that I knew I was a sinner and needed forgiveness. I asked Him to come into my life. I became a child of God. I entered into a relationship with the God of the universe. I didn't understand what having a relationship with God meant but I knew that what happened was real. I couldn't wait for Dad to get home for lunch so I could tell him about my decision. When he came in, Mom said, "Rachel has something to tell you." I was excited and felt a bit self-conscious, so I got him to bend down, and I whispered in his ear, "I asked Jesus into my heart." I don't remember that there was any reaction or response to my announcement.

Another way God's truths made their way into my mind was through hymns. Sunday morning, evening, and Wednesday night we were at church and there was always singing. I can still tell you the page numbers for some of the songs we sang regularly. I didn't understand all the truths I was ingesting but they were being stored up in my heart and mind. Years later they provided comfort during hard times and helped me refute the lies I had believed. There have been times as an adult when I heard or sang one of those hymns and understood for the first time the truth I had memorized so many years before.

Truth had always been right in the middle of the lies I believed. I didn't have any frame of reference to understand that God wanted me to have a relationship with Him. When I saw my parents reading their Bibles in the morning, they weren't checking off the "I read my Bible" box, they were talking to, listening to, and deepening their relationship with their Heavenly Father. The idea of reading my Bible as a means of developing a relationship with my Heavenly Father was something that couldn't be "caught." It was something that needed to be "taught." It was a long time before I learned how to read my Bible as a way to deepen my relationship with my Heavenly Father by listening to what He had to say in His Word.

Not Obedient Enough

Dear Mom,

You were always the best mom you knew how to be. However, like all parents you didn't always get it right and unfortunately this was the beginning of a lot of confusing and shameful thinking for me. I knew you didn't mean to but your methods of discipline added to my feelings of shame and inadequacy.

You had an almost obsessive desire for me to keep my dress down. I was always in a dress because one of your convictions was that girls should not wear pants. To this day I don't understand it. The only exception to that rule was when I was going to ride my bike. I could go put on my pedal pushers (now called capris) and go for a ride. Once I got off the bike, I had to go put my dress back on.

I was about eight years old when "keep your dress down" became something you said to me regularly. Usually, I would be sitting on the floor or crawling around on the sofa when I would experience the shame that came with the reprimand and look of disapproval. It wasn't that I didn't want to obey you; I was eight years old. I wasn't thinking about being ladylike. As I relived those moments I started to wonder if there had been something in your past that was triggered whenever I didn't "keep my dress down?" I can't know the answer to that question, but I do know what it did to me.

How does a little girl learn to do cartwheels, climb on the monkey bars, and a whole host of other activities in a dress? When I did get brave enough to try things on the neighbor's swing set you would get a call letting you know I had been showing off my underpants.

Things went from bad to worse when you added the threat, "If you don't start keeping your dress down, I'm going to buy you some bloomers to wear." The threat didn't give me the ability to magically remember to keep my dress down. One day you came home with some peach colored underwear that looked like what we now call bike shorts. They were not meant to be a fashion statement. Your intent was to shame me into keeping my dress down. It was not about giving me the freedom to be more active while not worrying about someone seeing my underwear. I don't know if you knew what happened in the backyard one day because of my bloomers.

I always wanted to climb up to the treehouse that Phil and Tim had built in the oak tree, but they would never let me. Not long after I started wearing the bloomers I was given the coveted invitation, "Rachel, do you want to climb up to the treehouse?" I quickly started to scramble up the ladder but before I got very far, I heard the boys laughing. My heart sank as I realized I had been fooled. They had just wanted to see my bloomers. Any joy I felt over the opportunity to climb the tree was obliterated.

To make matters worse I got a nickname. I became Pinky Lee. They even wrote a poem and would taunt me with it. "Pinky Lee, up a tree, so all can see, what's under me." And every time it was repeated the shame went deeper. I wonder if you knew about the poem. If you did why didn't you make them stop?

Feeling sad, Rachel

Boys Will Be Boys

I hadn't been the only one at my table during the *"Breaking Free From Body Shame"* class who had experienced shame and embarrassment from their brothers. During one of our table discussions one of the young ladies had told about being shamed by her brothers. I hadn't been very empathetic to her or to myself when I tried to discount the shame by saying, "boys will be boys." That had been true,

65

but it hadn't made it right and it hadn't taken away the shame and the pain.

During one of my sessions with Dawn, with tears streaming down my face I told her about my mother's obsession and the boy's trick. Dawn asked me, "How did that make Little Rachel feel?" I thought for a few minutes and said, "It made her feel betrayed and embarrassed by the boys. She also felt stupid for being fooled and unloved by her mother."

In her kind, gentle voice she then explained, "When events like this happen and there is no closure, they get filed in our memory with the emotion still attached to the event. When the memory is revisited the shame and humiliation are felt all over again. That's why there are tears." She continued, "When the event can be shared in a non-judgemental setting there can be closure and the event can be filed in our memory without the emotion still attached. Healing and forgiveness don't make the events that led to the shame and humiliation go away. The harm was real; it happened but it no longer has center stage. It has moved to the background." What a healing, freeing moment.

As I processed this new information from Dawn, I forgave Mom, because I understood that she hadn't known how to teach modesty in a way that didn't make me believe I was being bad. I also forgave the boys for their part in that painful situation and the hurtful poem that resurfaced from time to time over the years. When I thought about that event there were no tears and I didn't feel shame or humiliation – there had been healing. Before, it was center stage in my memory and there had been a spotlight on it. But now because it had moved to the background it had lost its power to bring shame.

I'm Here For Others

Dear Dad and Mom,

Being the Pastor's daughter wasn't easy for me. I "caught" quite a few lies as I tried to be who I thought I was supposed to be. In addition to thinking I needed to be perfect to get yours and God's approval, I thought it was my job to make other people comfortable. One of the ways that played out was the night the Batchelors (missionaries who had been staying with us over the weekend) *did a presentation for the Sunday evening church service. You remember they always had a table which contained memorabilia from the Samoan Islands, where they served. It was set up in front of the church on the left-hand side of the auditorium. Things like cooking utensils and decorative items the nationals made were on display. There were also some samples of the clothing the nationals wore. After sharing some stories about what was happening in Samoa they showed some slides. Next, they moved over to the table and started telling about each of the items that were on display. The congregation that had been spread across the three sections of pews started to move and gather around the front so they could see better. All of a sudden Mr. Batchlor said, "Rachel, will you come over here please?" I was nine years old and didn't think I could say no, so I went. They didn't explain what they were going to do or ask my permission. He and his wife just dressed me in the clothes that had been on the table. There I stood in front of the whole congregation of about seventy-five people who had gathered up front. I knew they were all looking at me and they were all laughing. I thought they were laughing at* **me.** *I felt very insecure, cornered, overwhelmed, exposed, vulnerable, extremely embarrassed and scared all at the same time. I was on the verge of tears and was thinking "I don't want to be here. Why are all these people laughing at me."*

Mom and Dad, I'm confident that you both had no idea what a traumatic experience that was for me.

I don't remember what happened next, but I do know that this event was seared into my memory. As a result, as much as possible I avoided being in any situation that would make me the center of attention with the possibility of feeling embarrassed or foolish. That is why the only sport I ever willingly participated in was soccer where I could "hide" in the backfield. No baseball – I would have to get up to bat. No volleyball – I would have to serve. I didn't have a choice about giving speeches in English class, but I would shake, my mouth would become dry, and I would have no facial expression. That was another place shame got into my life.

I want you to know healing has been happening. The time I've spent with Dawn and the books and articles I read have paid off. Recently when I attended the annual cookout for the senior's group at my church, my 73-year-old self was given an opportunity to tell the shame attendant, "You aren't going to get to keep stealing my joy." I signed up for and participated in the second annual Corn Hole Competition, something I had never done before. I realized that no one was sitting around laughing at the people who were participating and the people participating were having fun. I also realized that no one ever played the game perfectly. I had made the decision to participate before I left home that night.

It was time for the competition to begin, and I was standing beside my partner, Mary, still hoping I wasn't going to make a fool of myself. Not only was no one laughing at me, they weren't even paying any attention to me. I was feeling a bit more confident that win or lose it would be okay. Before the evening was over my partner and I had won first place in the women's competition. I even posed for a picture wearing the silly crown; not something I would have done in the past. That was great progress. Healing was happening. (However,

my old hip was not so happy. It took three trips to the
chiropractor to recover from the victory.)
    Love, Rachel

It's Not Okay to Cry

"Emotion is the energy around which the brain organizes itself."[39] When discussing how shame is attached to emotion, Dr Thompson said, "One way to approach its essence is to understand it as an undercurrent of sensed emotion, of which we may have either a slight or robust impression that, should we put words to it, would declare some version of I am not enough; There is something wrong with me; I am bad; or I don't matter.

But we would be mistaken if we thought that the story of shame begins with those words or that they tell it in its entirety. For although we come to understand much of who we are via the medium of language as a way to make sense of reality, our lives emerge most primarily in the forms of bodily sensations and movements, perceptions, and emotions. Emotion itself could be considered to be the gasoline in our human tank."[40] The shame attendant used the lies I had believed so that, just like my parents, my emotional tank stayed empty.

Dear Mom,

    We didn't show emotion very often in our house, did we? I
don't remember ever hearing you and Dad argue. If you did it
was behind closed doors. You once told me, "I can't show
you any sympathy because you fall apart." Message from the
shame attendant was received – It's not okay to cry. What this
actually meant was that there were emotions inside my
locked-up heart, but it wasn't okay to let them out. The next

---

[39] Thompson, The Soul of Shame, 50
[40] Ibid, 24

event in my story puts the spotlight on how this message played out in my life.

Fourth grade brought a couple of tragedies. I had made friends with a new girl in my class. Her family had immigrated from Poland, and they spoke very little English. Angela (not her real name) lived across the street from the school and every morning on my way to school I stopped at Angela's house so we could walk the rest of the way to school together. We did the same thing at lunch and after school. Mom, one day you came and gave me some very bad news. You said, "Angela was riding her bicycle down the street to the store, and she was hit by a car and killed." I didn't cry but when I went to bed that night, and for several nights after, I had a hard time sleeping because I could feel my heart pounding in my chest and I kept hearing my shame attendant whisper to me, "You never told her about Jesus." I was feeling guilt and shame on top of my grief. I didn't know what to do with any of those emotions. The lies I heard that night became part of my story.

It wasn't very long after that when one morning my teacher said, "Dennis won't be here today because his mother died." Dennis sat right in front of me and this news made my heart hurt. When Dennis came back to class, his eyes looked very sad, and I felt sad for him. It wasn't very long before Dennis didn't ever come back to school. My teacher said, "Dennis and his family have moved away." More sadness but no way to express it.

As I reflected on these events as an adult my heart hurt for my young self. Thinking about the guilt I felt for not sharing Jesus with Angela made me mad at my shame attendant. I had shown the love of Jesus to Angela by the way I had been a friend and had cared about her. I had lost two friends and there had never been anyone who shared my grief with me.

Just recently I was sharing these stories again and they still made me cry. Those events had gotten stored away with the unreleased emotion still attached. My heart still hurt because I hadn't been helped to grieve a very deep loss. I've now felt the pain of the loss and have learned to forgive both of you for not being able to help me grieve.

Mom, after I read an excerpt from a letter our family received after you died, I had a question for Dawn. During the next visit I read this statement to her, "Your mother had a tender empathetic heart and a sympathetic ear and sometimes one needed both. I've always counted it a privilege to have known her and to have her as a friend."

I asked Dawn, "Why could my mom be empathetic and sympathetic to others but not to me?"

She explained, "There are many factors that can contribute to a child experiencing a parent differently than others do. Some are the result of the closeness and familiarity of the relationship. It is safer for them to keep their distance when the relationship is close and familiar. Their parenting style, strict and authoritarian vs. friendly and more permissive also can play a role. The strict authoritarian parents would want the child to stay in control and not fall apart. Another reason is the parents may fear or be uncomfortable with a child's negative emotions. The parent's perceived role and responsibility in the life of the child vs. a friend or other family member can affect how they respond. For example, the sensation of responsibility to not coddle or spoil their child would not have been present with a friend. Also, the parents might not feel as competent to address a child's emotional needs as they would those of someone who are not as close since there is not as much responsibility."

She continued, "There are lots of other reasons, but it is not uncommon to notice a difference in a parent's patience, empathy, mercy, etc. for a friend or stranger vs. a child or spouse."

Any or all of those reasons could be why you didn't know how to validate my feelings and show me empathy or provide a way to let me express my feelings. I'm still sad that we didn't have a secure attachment and that you didn't know how to comfort me when I was sad. That can never be replaced but I do have a Heavenly Father who understands my pain and grief, and He knows how to "comfort all who mourn," (Isaiah 61:2) I have been learning how to let him.

Love, Rachel

So What?

The answer to the So What? for this chapter will be covered at the end of the next chapter.

CHAPTER SEVEN – STILL NOT PERFECT ENOUGH

Not Thin Enough

"I was always a fat child," I often said. When I looked at the pictorial timeline I had created starting at birth it didn't make sense. I could not find a single picture of a little fat girl. Pictures don't lie (this was pre-AI). That picture of cute two-year-old me playing in the dirt with my brother – nope, I hadn't been fat. I found one of my favorite pictures, my kindergarten school picture and guess what – I wasn't fat. I looked again at the picture of me when I was seven, the one that made me sad because I looked like I was afraid, you guessed it – not fat. There was one of me with my bike when I was ten and again - not fat. I was puzzled. What happened that had made me remember myself as being fat? I don't remember being teased or called fat by anyone. As I looked at the pictures, I remembered something that had happened when I was ten.

Dear Mom,

Do you remember the time Aunt Marion and cousin Lynda came to our house and brought me lots of clothes that Aunt Marion had made for Lynda? The first thing I saw was a beautiful poodle skirt in shades of purple and I was in love!!! To make it even better, there were lots of crinolines to wear underneath. I tried it on and there was a BIG problem – it didn't fit. Not one piece of clothing they brought me fit. I was devasted, ashamed and embarrassed. That was the day I started to believe that "I was fat."

I heard my shame attendant's voice say, "Lynda is four years older than you and the clothes fit her, but they don't fit you. That means you are fat." Mom, did you not realize the difference in our height and body type, and the fact that the clothes had been handmade by Aunt Marion specifically for Lynda would mean they weren't going to fit me? Even if I had been 10 pounds lighter the clothes would not have fit me, nor would they have complemented my body type.

*After they left, I kept looking at the clothes, especially the skirt, wanting it to fit, however, not only did the clothes not fit now, but they were also never going to fit. Instead of passing them on to someone who could wear them, you got the storage drum out of the closet and put all the clothes in it and put it back into the closet. This told me there was the expectation that **someday** I **should** be able to wear them.*

Time after time I pulled the drum out and dreamed of wearing the purple skirt. But time after time the clothes still didn't fit, and I felt the humiliation and shame all over again as I heard the voice of my shame attendant loudly say, "You are not thin enough. You are fat." I never wore any of those clothes. I never got to wear the purple skirt because I was too fat!

Sadly, Rachel

I'm Different

In addition to thinking I had to be perfect and that I should be further along and know more than I did, there was something else I "caught" in the parsonage; the belief that I was different. "The "I'm different" heresy comes from subtly being treated differently while you were growing up."[41]Dr Sandford wrote in his *"I Have To Be Perfect"* book, "You were under different rules. You had different expectations to

---

[41] Sanford, I Have To be Perfect, 51

74

live up to. These rules and expectations came from the forces of family and the church community."[42] Having rules that were different from my friends at school but also at church was confusing for me. However, because I was a rule follower I did my best to follow them even when I didn't understand. I didn't understand why it was wrong to dance, either.

As I researched my parents' past and learned about the culture of the twenties and thirties I understood a little bit more. Remember, I Thessalonians 5:22 instructed believers to "Abstain from every form of evil." (ESV) The speakeasies during Prohibition and Nightclubs from the 30's would all be places considered evil. I understood the need to abstain and how their convictions had developed. What I realized was that my parents had not known how to teach discernment. Therefore, their conviction about not dancing became my rule. I'm going to chat with them about that.

Dear Mom and Dad,

It was during my grade school years that your convictions, which had become my rules, started to highlight that I was different from all my friends and that added to my sense of shame.

One day I came home from school and told you about all the fun I had in music class that day. We learned to do the Hokey Pokey. That's when I found out there was no wiggle room in the rules. The Hokey Pokey was considered a dance and I was not allowed to participate. I was broken hearted.

Dr Thompson talks about the "shearing effect of shame."[43] I was simply participating in a new creative adventure and I was excited about it. Suddenly the "unexpected shearing effect" of shame stole my joy. I was

---

[42] Ibid, 51
[43] Thompson, The Soul of Shame, 65

deflated. I lowered my head and looked away. I wanted to ask why but that wasn't allowed.

It wasn't long after that event that the Maypole dance was being introduced in gym class. What a fun way to get exercise and learn coordination as we marched around the pole weaving those ribbons over and under until they were wrapped around the Maypole.

Dad, you have no idea how humiliated, confused and shame filled I was when I found out that you had gone to see the principal and had me excused from doing the Maypole. Instead, I had to sit on the gym floor with my back against the wall and watch all the fun. Once again there was no explanation except it was a dance and I wasn't allowed to dance. I have never been able to find anything evil in the Hokey Pokey either.

Next up in gym class was square dancing and another trip to the principal's office for you, Dad. This time I didn't even get to sit in the gym and watch the group. I had to sit in the locker room feeling left out and knowing I was different. When anyone asked about why I was not able to dance, the only thing I knew to say was "My dad's a preacher." And the neon "I'm different" sign would flash above my head.

How I wish you had been able to teach me about discernment; that all dance was not created equal. It was true that in many instances dancing took place in locations I shouldn't go. It was also true that dancing could lead to other things. That was part of the problem. You didn't talk about "other things" either and it was easier to just say no to all dancing and leave me with the belief that good Christians didn't dance. I was left feeling lonely, embarrassed, and left out. The truth was my friends never gave it another thought. They went on and danced and their feeling about me as their friend didn't change.

Love, Rachel

The Good Christian Box

The first eleven years of my life my faith narrative had been infiltrated with an inaccurate and incomplete view of God. I believed that God was disappointed with me and led to the lie that I could gain His approval by following the rules. I had not been taught how to be discerning, so my parents' convictions had become my rules. In my mind, I constructed my *Good Christian* box. Good Christians didn't drink, or go to movies, or play cards, or dance. They did read their Bible every day and pray. They also didn't miss church or get angry or depressed.

I believed that if I followed the rules and didn't color outside the lines, then my parents and God would be pleased with me. I believed that if the rules for being a good Christian were true for me they were also true for others and I became rigid and judgemental.

My faith narrative came from the unrealistic and inaccurate lies I "caught" at home and reinforced the walls of my *Good Christian* box. I internalized the lie that I was expected to be perfect and with that came the tyranny of the "I should…" and "I shouldn't…" thoughts. When I didn't do something I thought I should and vice versa, the shame attendant would usher me back into the box covered in more shame. That box kept me in bondage for most of my life.

During those years I was also "catching" how often my parents' served others. Our neighbors came to Mom for advice and help. I saw her learn to give shots so she could go across the street every four hours around the clock and administer morphine to Mr. Stone who was dying of cancer. I heard her talk to Johnny, who delivered our milk, about his need for Jesus. She stayed faithful when she had to have all of her teeth pulled and didn't get her dentures for a year. How embarrassing and hurtful that must have been, but it never stopped her from going to church and doing all of the things she always did.

Taking care of the people who came to our home, for a meal or an overnight, added to her already full plate taking care of her four children. I was in grade school before her clothes dryer wasn't a line strung across the backyard between the house and the garage. I don't remember ever hearing her complain. I saw her take care of Dad because she loved him and wanted to serve him, not because it was a duty or a chore. That was going to be very important for me later.

Dad was a good shepherd to his congregation. He made hospital visits and never neglected the older folks who couldn't come to church. There was a picture in the newspaper of him helping build a wheelchair ramp for one of the ladies at church.

While the shame attendant was at work in me, my parents' love for God and His Word was also evident even though it would be many years before I understood and appreciated them. The list of lies that had yet to be refuted with truth included the unspoken, unresolved sexual assault that had led me to believe I was bad. Mom's unwillingness to show me sympathy because I would "fall apart" along with the grief of losing friends with no way to process the loss led to the belief that it wasn't ok to cry. The shame and humiliation from the attempts to teach modesty, the humiliating experience at church and believing I was fat had all worked together to shape my inaccurate self-image.

The truth about God that had been written into my narrative was that He loved me enough to die on the cross for me. I had recognized my need of a Savior, and I was His child.

It was important to remember as I continued to excavate what I had learned from Dr Thompson – "What starts as a "simple" set of responses to nonverbal cues...as early as seven months eventually becomes what I tell myself silently or out loud in words, images and feelings about everything I believe about myself and the universe.[44] All the things I had caught and misinterpreted made up the story about me that I took with me as I entered Junior High.

So What?

Heavenly Father,

My journal entry reads, "You were good and faithful when Mr. Davies harmed me."

As I've been writing I've heard my shame attendant say many times, "So what, everyone has stuff in their lives, everyone will just think you are whining." He wanted me to believe the lie, accept the shame, and say, "You are right. I should just stop writing." But I know that Your message to me has been to write it down for Your honor and glory. I have continued to write, and I have continued the excavation in my search for truth. I have continued to re-story.

During this time in my life my brain had continued to develop, and my shame attendant had been hard at work filling my narrative with bad information. Daily I continue to hear his voice telling me that "I should already know" and "what I should do." The excavation work I've done is helping me recognize the lies more quickly. You know how Mom used to say, "You can't stop the birds from flying over your head, but you can keep them from building a nest in your hair." In II Corinthians 10:5 you say it this way, "We destroy arguments and every lofty opinion raised against the knowledge of God and take **every thought captive** (bold mine) to obey Christ."

I found one of your names that will help me to dismantle my *Good Christian* box. In Psalm 46:10 you tell me "Be still

---

[44] Thompson, The Soul of Shame, pg. 54

and know that I am God." A good translation is that I am to cease striving. You know that I have been striving for most of my life trying to get it right. That led to my feelings of inadequacy and guilt, and of course, shame. Your name Jehovah-mekoddishkem: The Lord Who Sanctifies You, helps me know that it's a lifelong process. The box started to crumble when I finally understood that I would never be able to make myself holy by following a set of dos and don'ts. It is You who makes me holy – sanctifies me, and it is You who gives me the desire to please You; not so I can earn anything, but because I belong to You. Salvation came to me as a free gift. I can rest from trying to be good enough.

I am reminded again of Your promises from Jeremiah 29:13 "You will seek me and find me, when you seek me with all your heart, and from Psalm 147:3 "He heals the broken hearted and binds up their wounds." (ESV)"

I am finding You and You are binding up my wounds, and I am loving You more every day.

Thank You, Jesus, for saving me and for loving me.

Amen

CHAPTER EIGHT – ADOLESENCE

For the LORD sees not as man sees man looks on the outward appearance, but the LORD looks on the heart. (I Samuel 16:7)

My World Was Small

The video screen in front of me displayed the progress of my flight to Hawaii and the blue dot I saw in the middle of the Pacific Ocean was my destination. *In just a couple of hours I am going to be just a dot on that dot*, I thought and immediately felt very insignificant. I quickly recognized that was my shame attendant telling me a lie. Everything I had learned so far on my journey to healing and wholeness said differently.

God's omniscience and His omnipresence meant that He knew me, and He was with me right there in the airplane. *God not only knows me, but He knows every person on this plane, every person on the planet as well as every person that has ever lived or ever will live,* my thoughts continued as I felt overwhelmed. My finite mind could not begin to fathom my infinite God. My life in my small world had not been unseen or insignificant in the eyes of my Heavenly Father. Even though there had been some healing and I was learning to forgive I kept digging. I was going to discover how the wounds of early childhood impacted my junior high and high school years. This search also led to finding some new wounds.

If Hawaii had been just a dot, then Hammond, Indiana was dot dust. When I looked at a map and calculated how far my school, my church, my friends, the grocery store, and downtown had been from my house, it didn't take me long to find out that all of those places had been within five miles of my home. Geographically my world had been very, very small. My spiritual life had been reduced to my *Good Christian* box. I knew nothing about what was happening around the world. My friends all lived in my neighborhood, or I knew them from church. Conclusion, I was naïve, had been very sheltered and my *Good Christian* box was intact when it was time for junior high.

Moving Up

Summer was over. It was the fall of 1963. I was going to be twelve in just a few weeks, and I was going to Gavit Junior High taking all my wounds and shame with me. What better place than junior high for the shame attendant to show up and remind me of my insecurities. Most of my classmates, that I had been with since kindergarten, were going to a different junior high. As a result, I was starting fresh as a small fish in a big pond of approximately 1,500 junior high and high school students in the same building.

I became acquainted with many of my classmates but only developed a relationship with two of them. Joy sat in front of me in homeroom. Our lockers were beside each other and we shared our faith. Our friendship lasted throughout high school and she was the only friend with whom I ever had contact after graduation. I don't remember how Donna and I became friends. I know that I spent enough time around her that I picked up her favorite bad word, and with it, condemnation from my shame attendant every time the word crossed my lips. To this day that word will occasionally slip out.

Call waiting had not yet been invented. The possibility of an emergency call for Dad meant that we were not allowed to hang out on the phone talking to friends. The only contact I had with my two friends was at school.

Not Good Enough

Gym class offered many opportunities for my shame attendant to add to my "not good enough" narrative. In grade school I hadn't had to change clothes or take a shower for gym class but that changed in junior high and high school. Every day when I stood in the locker room in my little changing booth hiding behind the curtain trying not to be seen while I put on my ugly blue gym suit, I heard the "not thin enough" lie. I won't even mention the humiliation attached to the memories of the showers.

The Presidential Fitness Test had been established in 1956 by President Dwight D. Eisenhower.[45] It had been designed to assess cardiovascular fitness, upper-body and core strength, endurance, flexibility, and agility. Riding a bicycle and reading books had not prepared me for this test. I wasn't the weakest or the slowest but there were plenty of opportunities for my shame attendant to discourage me as I compared myself to others and always came up "not good enough." Even Dad and Mom believed I was "not good enough" since gym was the only class where it was acceptable to have a C on my report card.

One particularly traumatizing event happened during my freshman year. We were introduced to gymnastics. The uneven parallel bars and the balance beam were the two events that can still give me nightmares. At the end of the grading period, we were required to "perform" in front of the whole class on the balance beam. It was my turn. I managed to get up on the beam and as I gingerly made my way across, I lost my balance and fell off. As I fell to the right, my left leg

---

[45] https://en.wikipedia.org/wiki/Presidential_Fitness_Test

caught the beam, stayed to the left, and dislocated my knee. Shame and embarrassment flooded me when I hobbled off the mat.

Since we didn't have family health insurance and the school insurance hadn't been purchased, I wasn't taken to the doctor. After about a week I went back to school even though my knee was still very swollen and painful.

My teacher, Miss Kelly, called me into her office because she had noticed that I was still limping. She was not happy when she found out I hadn't been to see a doctor. She told me that after this much time my knee should have been doing better. She said, "You need to tell your parents that you need to see a doctor."

"Mom, Miss Kelly said that I need to see a doctor because my knee should be better by now." An appointment was made and after the doctor examined my knee he ordered x-rays. He came back into the room and put the x-rays up on the light box. "The dislocation caused a bone to chip inside Rachel's knee," he explained. "We don't know where the chipped piece is but if it is still behind her knee, it could move and cause her knee to lock up permanently. The only way to determine if it is in there is to aspirate the fluid from her knee. We will then put the aspirated fluid into a bowl and, if after a few minutes it looks like there is grease floating on top of the fluid, it will mean the bone has chipped and it will mean surgery." The aspiration was done, the look of grease showed up, and the surgery was scheduled. Guilt and shame for my clumsiness causing financial stress on the family became my constant companions.

I wore a cast from mid-thigh to my ankle for six weeks and required crutches. My friend Joy was driven to school by her mother every day. They offered to drive by our house and pick me up. One positive thing, I was given a key to the school elevator and I didn't have to manage the steps to the second floor.

The next year when Dad was doing his taxes, I got a bit of relief from my guilt of causing financial problems for the family. After Dad finished his taxes he came to me and patted me on the shoulder and called me his "little tax deduction." That helped some with the guilt but the shame of being clumsy continued.

Music – Good and Bad

When I was in seventh grade my oldest brother, Phil, gave me a wonderful gift. I'm going to tell him about it.

Dear Phil,

I remember the day the piano came into our house. You were in choir at school and admired the choir director. You even decided that you were going to learn to play the piano. You had a job, so you bought an upright piano. If my memory serves me right (sometimes it doesn't) the piano cost $60.00. Rather quickly after you started taking lessons you decided it wasn't what you really wanted to do with your time, and you quit. I'm so thankful that instead of selling the piano, you paid for my lessons. It is one of the greatest gifts I ever received, and those lessons have served me well throughout my life.

Thankfully, Rachel

The piano was located in the living room and near the kitchen. That was a perfect setup for my shame attendant. I'm going to talk to Mom about that.

Dear Mom,

When Ruth also started taking lessons it provided another opportunity for my shame attendant to show up. Every time you shared what our piano teacher had told you, "Ruth's ability comes naturally. Rachel works for everything she gets," my shame attendant was right there shouting "Not good enough!"

The piano was in the living room right off the kitchen and I hated to practice because every time I hit a wrong note (which was often) you would make a groaning sound. That sound equated to "not good enough" from the shame attendant. I already knew I had made a mistake. You didn't have to make that irritating sound. I continued to practice but didn't get much better. It was another thing the shame attendant regularly brought to mind.

Years later when doing an abilities evaluation I scored low on Tonal Memory. The report said, "May have difficulty in remembering tunes and tonal sequences. This ability is used to sing and play music by ear." The teacher had been right. I did have to work for what I got. The shame attendant had exploited what should have been an accomplishment.

Remembering, Rachel

Even though the tonal memory didn't help with the piano playing, I did have good singing ability and Mom nurtured it. An addition had been built on our house and the piano had been moved down the hall to the sitting room by her bedroom. She had a subscription for a music book that came once a quarter. Every time the new one arrived she sat down at the piano and played through some of the new songs to find which ones would be good for me to sing. After I learned one it wasn't long before I would sing it at church. As I thought about this, I wondered why I was able to be vulnerable and sing at church, but I was so afraid to risk other activities where I was in front of people. I decided it was because I had no fear of being laughed at when I sang at church.

Even though I hadn't realized it as a teenager, music helped me build a relationship with God. It was through the songs I learned to sing for and with others in church that I learned more about God's attributes. I learned about his faithfulness and that I could trust Him. Those songs were imbedded in my heart and mind, and my relationship grew one song at a time. I didn't see it, but God did. The shame attendant saw it too, and he didn't want me to recognize it. He wanted me to keep thinking I was a disappointment to God.

I needed to talk to Mom and Dad both about the good and bad of being part of the choir at school.

Dear Mom,

Remember when I had been one of the four girls chosen to sing a solo in the concert choir Spring Concert? I was so excited about it. All of the songs for the concert had been popular when our soldiers were getting ready to leave for WWII. The guys wore military uniforms, and the girls wore long fancy dresses. It was supposed to have been very romantic and sad.

You were fine with me singing but you sure didn't want me to hold hands with the boy as I sang "When The Deep Purple Falls" to him. So instead of it being a joyful time celebrating my accomplishment it became a place for my shame attendant to shear my joy. You did relent and I did hold the boy's hand. However, I knew the night of the concert that you were sitting in the audience with a look of disapproval on your face.

Sadly, Rachel

Dear Dad,

You had no idea how much it wounded my heart and made me think you didn't love me when you didn't attend any of my concerts. The shame attendant knew, and he reminded me many times through the years about the disappointment and hurt I felt when you didn't come to hear me sing.

As I thought about this wound it made me think about how in the garden Satan got Eve to question God. There was only one tree in the whole garden that was off limits, but he used that tree to tempt Eve. In the almost eighteen years I lived at home and the hundreds of things you did for me over those years, Dad, my shame attendant used the eight times you didn't go to my concerts to make me think you didn't love me.

Mr. Clark, our choir director, was also the organist at his church. Many of the songs we sang were religious. During the year we would go to different churches and perform. I was so surprised when I asked you to let us come and sing at our church and you said "yes." That was the only time during the four years I sang in the school choir that you heard me perform with the choir.

In preparation for those concerts, the week before, we would go to the church where we were going to perform and practice during our choir period. Many of the students drove to school and on those practice days everyone got in someone's car and headed to the church. Dad, you wouldn't let me ride with any of my friends. Instead, you would come to school, pick me up, take me to the church, and wait in the car until we were finished.

When your brother was my age, he had been in a serious car wreck and was on the operating table for hours getting glass picked out of his face. I wonder if that had anything to do with your decision to not let me ride in cars with my friends. I wouldn't know because I wasn't allowed to ask. This time my shame attendant used the lie that everyone was going to think something bad about me. The truth was they didn't even care or notice.

I was chosen to be part of the Madrigal, the smaller group from the choir that sang music from the Renaissance period. Your convictions about alcohol created another place for my shame attendant to show up. We had been asked to sing outside of school hours for a civic club. They were meeting at a local restaurant. However, because the restaurant sold alcohol you wouldn't let me participate.

You and Mom weren't home that evening as I waited on the back porch for my friend who was going to pick me up. I had decided I was going to go anyway. My mind was racing trying to convince myself to just go and deal with the consequences. But when my friend pulled up, I went to her car and told her I couldn't go. She didn't think anything of it. She just said, "Okay," and left without me. My teacher probably didn't even notice I wasn't there. But I can still feel the conflict of frustration, anger and fear that went on in my mind. My shame attendant said, "You're different. You have to follow rules no one else does. It's not fair."

You were loving me the best way you knew how and I love you for that.

Rachel

More Lies for The Box

My Senior year I attended a church sponsored winter retreat. The speaker, Sketch Erickson, was a chalk artist. The top sheet of paper on his easel had a drawing of a radio sitting on top of a stove with musical notes floating around it and the title, "What's Cooking On Your Radio?" We had all been taught that Rock and Roll was evil. Sketch said, "Some of you will tell me that you don't listen to the words; you just like the music." He turned on an instrumental recording of some popular tunes and watched as all of us started mouthing the words. He made his point that we couldn't just listen to the music; we also learned the words. I don't remember how he concluded his talk, but my shame attendant made sure I left with a load of guilt and shame even though I didn't know why. In my sheltered world it was many years before I had any understanding of what had been wrong with the words of some of the Rock and Roll songs. As I looked at the list of the top 100 singles of 1969, I understood what my parents' concerns had been. I just wish they had been able to help me learn how to discern the good from the bad back then.

In the back of the Bible I used at that time, I found a list of the scripture verses that were intended to be the proof texts for why Rock and Roll was wrong. I had the list, but they were never explained or discussed. An open discussion of the sexual references and inuendo in the songs would have required an open, honest discussion about sex. As I mentioned before, that never happened either. From my perspective it appears that once again it had just been easier for them to say all of it was wrong.

Along with the list of verses in the back of my Bible that were supposed to prove why not to listen to Rock and Roll there had been three other lists: one for dancing; one for movies; and one for dating. Saying no to those three things became a part of my *things not to do* checklist in my *Good Christian* box. I wasn't able to tell anyone why it made you a good Christian if you didn't dance or go to movies, but I didn't dance and I didn't go to movies. There had been some truth in the rules, and there had also been a matter of preference. The verses that were not on my "proof text" list were the most important and would have been the perfect teaching tool for all of the "don'ts.*" Philippians 4:8-9 "...whatever is true, whatever is honorable, whatever is just, whatever is pure, whatever is lovely, whatever is commendable, if there is any excellence, if there is anything worthy of praise, think about these things."* However, without knowing how to discern I had learned to stay in the box and not color outside the lines. On the rare occasion that I did decide to color outside the lines the decision came with guilt and shame.

Changes in the World Around Me

Mom and Dad never initiated any discussions about segregation, civil rights, or anything political. As time passed the makeup of residents of the Center had changed. It was no longer a place where people lived while they found jobs, became able to be self-supporting, and then move out of the Center. Many of the families who lived there became stuck in the cycle of poverty. It grieved me when I realized that, from my perspective, the church had quit reaching out to that community as it changed.

In the past my Mom had befriended our neighbors across the street who lived in the Center. That had changed and even though we knew their names, we didn't play with the kids from that side of the street. Mom no longer connected with the families as she had in the past. I didn't cognitively understand this change. It had definitely been a "caught not deliberately taught" experience. I was no longer allowed to "cut through" the Center on my way to church because, even though there were no facts to support the idea, it was deemed to be dangerous. I had been learning to be prejudiced toward anyone or anything that was different. That included race, socioeconomic status, culture, and religion. My *Good Christian* box had added prejudice and had unintentionally become more rigid.

There were changes going on in the world outside my home that made my dad become more protective, but there were no discussions about those changes. I felt a pervasive sense of fear. The Civil Rights movement, the Vietnam war and the counterculture had all happened right outside my door, and I had been clueless. It was many years before I was able to recognize the extent of my parents' prejudice and how I had become infected as well. I confessed and repented of my prejudice. I started making a concerted effort to immerse myself in other cultures. I wanted to learn and appreciate them with the hope of tearing down the walls I had unknowingly constructed and had wounded my heart. Healing for my wounded heart came from learning and understanding the truth.

Not Thin Enough

The belief that I was fat continued as I entered puberty. My body shape developed earlier than many of my peers. I was taller, had broader shoulders and I looked much older than I was. A Bible College choir was going to be performing at our church and some of the students were staying in our home. "What are you going to be doing now that you are out of school?" one of the students asked. Having just graduated from the eighth grade I replied, "I think I'll go to high school."

I recently showed someone my eighth-grade graduation picture and asked them, "How old do you think I was?" He replied, "Seventeen or eighteen." I was only thirteen.

My parents had been in their mid-fifties when I was in junior high and each began to have some health problems. When I was fourteen dad had a heart attack and was in the hospital. I dressed up (which would have included high heels) and took the bus downtown to go visit him. The bus driver thought I was on my way to work and wanted me to pay full fare.

Not Smart Enough

One of my electives my senior year was an office machines class. I was doing fine on the ten key adding machine. Then we advanced to a more complex machine. (I can still see the monster in my mind, but I don't know what it was called). No one knew I was struggling and not turning in my work.

I was an assistant in the Social Studies Office during my study hall periods. Part of my responsibility in the Social Studies Office was to go to the office machines classroom and make copies of tests on the mimeograph machine (Xerox wasn't around yet). The teacher of my office machines class was friends with the head of the Social Studies Department. They decided that until I got caught up in my office machines class I was no longer allowed to go there and make copies. I don't remember any discussion about why I wasn't doing well or any offer of help.

Apparently, I wasn't the only one who struggled in that class. By the end of the semester all we had to do to pass was turn in our assignments. There was a large bin in the room where we just threw in our work. I didn't know how to use that monster machine, but I did know how to use the ten key adding machine to get the same answer. The work turned in wasn't checked for accuracy but just checked to see if it was there. I passed the class, but not without reminders from the shame attendant that I should have been able to figure it out. And, if I should have been able to figure it out then it wasn't ok to ask for help.

Believing that "I should already know…" was the lie that led to not being able to ask for help. Freshman year I took Algebra. Math and I were not friends. My brother Tim was very good at math, and I asked him to help me. He sat down at the kitchen table with me as I struggled through the first story problem. We moved on to the next one and I had no idea how to figure it out. Tim stood up, slammed the book shut and said, "Boy, you're dumb," as he left the room. So much for asking for help.

My shame attendant tried many times to get me to quit writing this book. I continued to hear that voice inside my head that said, *"Your life wasn't so bad. There are many people who have had it far worse."* I also heard it say, *"They are just going to think you are whining."* The one I heard most often was, *"You don't have anything to say that hasn't already been said."*

A quote from Brené Brown explains why I didn't listen and kept writing, "Shame hates having words wrapped around it. If we speak shame, it begins to wither. …language and story bring light to shame and destroy it."[46] I was on a quest to uncover the sources of my shame, and I wasn't going to stop telling my story and shine the light of truth on my shame.

Happily Ever After

Since we didn't have television, reading was my only form of entertainment. I enjoyed reading about romance and did not know that these stories with their happily ever after themes were creating unrealistic expectations about what a healthy romantic relationship should look like. When I was in sixth grade the girls had been shown a movie about getting your period and that was the only information I had about growing up physically.

At the age of sixteen during my senior year I had my first boyfriend. At Christmas time that year the fifteen-year-old brother of the lady for whom I babysat was visiting from out of state. We spent time together during his visit and when he went back home, we started writing to each other. I'm sure that if I had those letters now, I would be mortified by what my romantic sixteen-year-old self-had written. Dad was concerned about the relationship because of the differences in our upbringing and culture. His prejudice was showing. I was supposed to stop writing to him. But I didn't. I would drop my letters in the big blue mailbox as I passed it on the way to school. He would send my letters to his sister's house. It was

---

[46] Brené Brown, Daring Greatly, pg. 67

my one act of outright rebellion and disobedience and the one thing I never confessed to them. It was also a source of guilt and shame over the years.

When school was out, he came back to spend the summer with his sister. He didn't have a car, so we didn't go on dates. We did go to youth activities together and sat in church together. I was with him at his sister's house one afternoon when I got my first kiss. His seven-year-old niece witnessed the kiss and before long she told my mother. I remember the day I came home and realized that she knew. I could tell that she wasn't happy, but I didn't know why. She asked me about the kiss, and I knew she was disappointed in me. There had never been any discussion about dating behavior in the past and there was no further discussion about it then, but the look she gave me definitely sheared off any joy I had experienced from that first kiss.

Other than in the romantic letters we exchanged we never discussed anything about a future together. What could that have looked like? He still had another year of high school and lived in another state twelve hours away. I had three years of college. Any idea of a future for us was pure fantasy. However, I had no idea how deeply he was invested in a future with me.

One evening as it was getting close to time for me to leave for school and for him to go back home, we were sitting together on my front porch. As we sat there, I said, "If anyone should ask me for a date after I get to school, I'm going to say yes." That statement wounded him. His sister told me later that when he got back to her house, he was so upset he punched the wall and told her, "She said she is going to date."

I left for school. He went back home, and we continued to write letters. But it wasn't long before I told him, in a letter, that I wasn't going to write anymore. Many, many years later in a discussion with his sister she told me again that I had broken his heart. My first thought was *That was over fifty years ago, he needs to get over it.* Knowing now what unresolved wounds can do to a heart, it makes me sad to know how deeply he had been wounded by my rejection. What I didn't see was that he really liked me just the way I was. Even though I thought I was fat it didn't matter to him. What the shame attendant wanted me to hear now was, "You should have known…" I was not mature enough in anyway to have known my disobedience to my parents would have such consequences. This is one example of when Dad's protective nature would have saved a lot of heartbreak.

Faith

When I had heard that whisper "Rachel I've always known your heart," what did it mean during those adolescent years? As I thought about this as an adult, I knew that anytime I "heard" God speaking to me what I heard had to match up with Scripture. I remembered a story in I Samuel 16 when God sent the prophet Samuel with instructions for anointing the next king. He was to go to Jesse the Bethlehemite to find the next king among his sons.

When he saw the oldest son Eliab verse 6 says, "…he looked on Eliab and thought, "Surely the LORD's anointed is before him."

But God responded, "Do not look on his appearance or on the height of his stature, because I have rejected him. For the LORD sees not as man sees: man looks on the outward appearance, but the LORD looks on the heart." (vs 7) There was the proof that I could trust that God sees my heart.

The word translated as **heart** from the original Hebrew into English in the Bible is used 252 times and is defined as "inner man, mind, will, heart, soul, understanding".[47] The

---

[47] https://www.blueletterBible.org/lexiCOn/h3824/kjv/wlc/0-1/

same word found in Jeremiah 29:13 that says, "You will seek me and find me, when you seek me with all your heart."

The shame attendant is known for taking truth and twisting it just a bit. Remember when he asked Eve in Genesis 3:1, "Did God *actually* (italics mine) say, "You shall not eat of any tree in the garden?" As an adolescent living in the *Good Christian* box I believed that having a "Quiet Time" was at the top of the list of things "I Should" do. Psalm 1:2, "...but his delight is in the law of the Lord, and on his law, he meditates day and night." This Psalm along with many other scriptures taught me the importance of spending time in God's Word. What I didn't know was that there were no scriptures with a required "Quiet Time" plan. That was a lie from the shame attendant. When the idea of "Quiet Time" was presented to me, what I heard was that I should spend every morning, same time, same place, and it should last about thirty minutes to an hour reading my Bible and praying.

There were reasons why meeting with God first thing in the morning was a good habit to develop but there weren't any rules. The same components that made up a good relationship with friends and family also made for a good relationship with my Heavenly Father. Relationships are fluid. They all require time, trust, commitment, faithfulness, conversation, gut level sharing, and accountability to flourish. They aren't rules to follow.

I was also given a prescription for prayer. Use of the acronym – ACTS – Adoration, Confession, Thanksgiving and Supplication was to be part of my prayer every time and in that order. The time and place and how to pray were intended to be a template, not a mandate, but my brain didn't receive them that way. The goal of a "Quiet Time" should have been to spend time with Jesus developing a relationship with him. There were so many resources out there that would have helped me learn what to do but I didn't have any of those.

What I did have was my shame attendant telling me I was disappointing God.

What the shame attendant didn't want me to know and understand was that even though I wasn't having the prescribed "Quiet Time," I was in a relationship with Jesus and He wasn't disappointed with me. I was doing what Psalm 119:11 said, "I have stored up your Word in my heart, that I might not sin against you."

Let's Wrap This Up

During my four years of high school my parents both had heart attacks. My mom had also gone to work outside the home which left me with more responsibility. My oldest brother, Phil, had joined the Army, gotten married and was serving in Vietnam. My brother, Tim, had moved to Connecticut for an apprenticeship with Pratt & Whitney Aircraft. In early August before I left for college he got married. As I was leaving home my sister Ruth was starting high school.

It was the end of August of 1969 and ready or not I was leaving home for college. My *"Good Christian"* box was solid. It was also very full of information I hadn't yet learned how to use and apply.

When it came time to pick a college that decision was made for me because:

1.) The three year Bible Institute Dad had chosen for me to attend was affordable.

2.) Dad knew the president.

3.) The school was a member of the IFCA.

4.) My lifelong friend, Kathy, who was the daughter of a pastor friend of Dad, was also going. (Our parent's met when our moms were pregnant with us. We had known each other all of our lives.)

"You don't have to go, but if you go you have to stay," Dad had told me. We loaded up the car and drove the 500 miles from northern Indiana to West Virginia.

My wounded and broken heart along with my shame attendant went with me and made sure to keep reminding me that: I needed to be perfect; I was fat; there were many things that I should already know but didn't; and that God was disappointed with me.

Saying Goodbye

Dear Mom and Dad,

When I first started reading Dr Thompson's book I didn't understand when he said that shame wasn't merely an emotion that led to such words as "I'm bad" but that it was the "primary tool that evil leverages, out of which emerges everything we would call sin."[48] What did that mean? How could my wounds be considered sin? The excavation process helped me figure it out. Wounds that aren't addressed fester both physically and emotionally. When I left home with my emotional wounds still intact, attached to them were bitterness, resentment, and pride, all sin.

My shame attendant had been doing his best to use his shovel to kill, steal and destroy my relationship with God. But God had been at work using His shovel to keep that from happening. Your lives taught me about God's faithfulness and that I could trust him. Those two things were going to get me through many things over the next years. So, even though I was unprepared in so many ways my foundation was firm. God knew me and He knew my heart. His purpose for me was to be conformed to the image of His son.

---

[48] Thompson, The Soul of Shame pg. 22

As I say goodbye to you, I am taking all you taught, good and bad, with me into this next chapter. I'm ready to keep digging and see what I can learn.

Your daughter, Rachel

So What?

Heavenly Father,

What I discovered from this layer of excavation was that while my brain had been developing and making it possible for me to learn to make decisions, set goals and manage my thoughts and emotions, my environment did not encourage me to use any of those skills.

You knew that not being able to express opinions, ask questions, or be part of the decision making process kept me from growing in those areas. In addition, the "emotional neglect" with the help of my shame attendant had left me having difficulty asking for help, feeling like a fraud, and being disappointed with myself. You knew that all of those things were going to be true. And You knew that I believed the same thing about myself spiritually.

I had gained knowledge about you, God, but I hadn't deepened in my understanding of what it meant to be in relationship with You. My shame attendant was quick to point this out as a failure on my part.

The name that helped me understand and extend grace to myself is Jehovah-raah: The Lord is My Shepherd. I heard You, my Shepherd, that night in class when you told me you had always seen my heart. You knew the conflicting information I had received and the struggle it caused me. Yet You tenderly kept calling my name and guiding me into paths of righteousness.

Instead of being covered in shame because I didn't have a deep enough relationship with You, I was able to tell a different story. I was developing a relationship with the God of the universe, and it was a lifelong process. I wasn't a failure and I wasn't a disappointment. I was doing exactly what II Peter 3:18 said I was supposed to do. "Grow in the grace and knowledge of our Lord and Savior Jesus Christ." So, I'm going to keep digging.

Thanks for loving me.

Amen

CHAPTER NINE – COLLEGE

...the sweetness of a friend is better than self-counsel
Proverbs 27:9b

Friendships

The campus was nestled in the beautiful mountains of Southern West Virginia. My parents, my sister and I arrived on campus in the late afternoon and made our way across the gravel parking lot, up the long awkward set of steps, to the girl's dorm.

My friend Kathy and her family arrived about the same time. Kathy and I were very happy that our rooms were right beside each other. (No freshmen were allowed to share a room.) Our dad's backed the cars to the side entrance and the boxes and suitcases were carried into our rooms. Once that task was completed, we loaded up the cars and went in search of a place to eat.

We found the Shoney's Big Boy and enjoyed our last meal together and were returned to campus. We hugged one more time before they got back in their cars and drove away. I can still see Kathy and me sitting on the rock wall at the bottom of the driveway watching the cars pull out of the parking lot feeling lonely and a bit scared as the taillights faded away into the distance. We slowly made our way up the steep driveway toward the dorm. We had roommates to meet and unpacking to do.

At five minutes till seven the next morning I stood in the hallway waiting for Kathy (the only person I knew) so we could go to breakfast together. At five minutes till seven

Becky stood in the hallway waiting for Carolyn (the only person she knew) so they could go to breakfast. This happened several days in a row. Becky and I quit waiting for Kathy and Carolyn and headed off to breakfast without them. A new lifelong friendship with Becky was born in the hallway of Des Plaines Hall in the fall of 1969.

That Boy

There were about 60 students in the freshman class that year. This was more than any of the classrooms could hold so we met in what had become the dining hall/chapel/classroom. *That boy needs somebody to iron his shirts*, I thought as I looked at the young man sitting in front of me every day. I didn't know that I was going to be the "somebody" who ironed his shirts for many years. Listen in as "that boy" introduces himself.

My name is Carl Wayne Stewart. I went by my middle name because I shared the first names of my dad, Carl, and my grandfather, Wayne. For many years we lived close enough to my grandparents that I became known as "Little Wayne." I was born in Beckley, West Virginia in March of 1951. I was the oldest of the four Stewart children; Wayne, Donna, Lynn, and Greg. My dad was in the Navy when I was born. As a result, for the first two years of my life it was just me and my mom. I was five and my sister, Donna, was three when our dad was discharged from the Navy and returned to Beckley to rejoin our family.

Soon after his discharge my dad enrolled in college planning to become a teacher. My grandmother had started teaching school in a one room schoolhouse when she was sixteen. She decided that it would be a good time for her to go to college and get her teaching degree, too. Together they commuted the sixty miles to Morris Harvey College in Charleston, West Virginia. Mother and son graduating together was commemorated in a newspaper article that included a picture of me, "Little Wayne," wearing a graduation cap sitting between my dad and my grandmother.

It didn't take long for my dad to realize that teaching was not going to be for him. Instead, he got a job working for the Social Security Administration. I was seven when my dad took his first assignment that took our family from Beckley, West Virginia to Logan, West Virginia. I had a very hard time with the idea of leaving Beckley. My grandmother was my school teacher. She had to bribe me with a new winter coat so I would be willing to make the move. While we were living in Logan my mom gave her life to Christ.

Pikeville, Kentucky was the next stop for my family when dad got another promotion. I was twelve and I thrived in the idyllic neighborhood where we lived. It didn't matter if it was my house or not, if I was hungry or thirsty just like all the other kids in the neighborhood I was welcome to go into any house and help myself to a sandwich and/or a drink. My mom's name was Iona, but everyone called her Oni. Famous in the neighborhood for her bologna sandwiches, she earned the nickname Oni Baloney.

My new best friend Bobby and I spent a lot of time in my downstairs bedroom. We had a big refrigerator box set up under the stairs that we used for target practice with our BB guns. Donna had a crush on Bobby. She and her best friend Michele decided it would be a good idea to go downstairs, hide in the box, and eavesdrop on Bobby and me. All was going well until we started shooting at the box. The girls tried to stay quiet but finally had to reveal themselves. Besides getting hit with some BB's they got in a lot of trouble for that stunt.

When I was in the tenth grade there was another move. My dad got another promotion and became the manager of the Charleston, West Virginia Social Security Office. The house our family moved into was in Elkview right along the Elk River about fifteen miles from Dad's office. Now instead of shooting BB's at refrigerator boxes, river rats were the target. Elkview Baptist Church was right beside our house and for the first time the family started attending church together.

I was sixteen when one Sunday night my dad and I responded to the pastor's message and walked up to the front of the church to talk to the pastor. Everyone had been praying for both of us and they were very excited when we indicated an interest in surrendering our lives to Christ. Soon after, Dad and I were baptized.

I later realized that I had not truly surrendered my life to Christ that night. The person who talked to me when I walked the aisle did not do a good job of determining where I was in my search for God. So even though I "prayed the prayer" and got baptized I wasn't a believer.

I liked girls and the girls liked me. Good Baptist girls did not date boys who weren't good Baptist boys. No one realized that I had not become a good Baptist boy that night when I walked the aisle, so it was okay when I started dating one of the Baptist girls. I attended church and youth group so I could be with my girlfriend. I kept hearing more about what a relationship with Jesus looked like, but I was unintentionally living a double life. I tried to be Wayne, the Christian, but that conflicted with the Wayne who loved to dance, smoke and drink.

My sister Donna told a funny story about what it was like to be my sister. One night she and her friend Vivian went to the Drive Inn with me. I had Donna move over into the driver's seat and I took off to be with my friends. Donna enjoyed pretending that she was the driver but when the movie was over and all the cars had left, she and Vivian were still sitting there in the car. The man who was running the place told Donna they needed to move their car. She didn't know how to drive so he moved the car outside the gate for her. While they waited for me, they decided it would be a great time and place to practice driving. The Drive Inn was beside an abandoned railroad and there was a wide dirt road between the railroad and the Drive Inn. The girls took turns driving up and down that road as they waited for me to come back. I told them that I wanted to get back sooner but the people I left with wouldn't bring me back.

Not for the first time, I was stopped by the police one night. This time I had been drag racing on a motorcycle, going the wrong way, and under the influence. When the officer recognized me, he said, "Not you again." That was the night I lost my license until I turned twenty-one.

It was two years later, in 1968 at the church's winter retreat that I recognized I had not surrendered my life to Christ that night when I was sixteen. I was lying in my bunk, and I experienced the convicting power of the Holy Spirit. It was that night that I surrendered my life to Christ. That was the night that my life changed. Instead of wanting to drink, and smoke and run around I wanted to tell others about Jesus.

In the Spring of 1969, I attended a college preview at the Bible Institute. Later that year the men's quartet from the school was at my church. One of the members of the quartet joined our family for a meal and spent time talking with me about attending the school. In the fall of 1969 instead of taking a full ride baseball scholarship to Morris Harvey College I enrolled at the Bible Institute. I was the boy who needed someone to iron his shirts and who became part of a group of friends that included Rachel and lasted the rest of our lives.

Rachel Gets Homesick

The first six weeks at school had been really hard for me. We were not allowed to go home during those first weeks. With the exception of overnights at girlfriends' houses, the one week of summer camp I had attended in grade school, and a weekend choir trip in high school, I had never been away from home over night. Now I was five hundred miles away and I was extremely homesick. The teacher who recognized my homesickness, reached out, and became my friend, she was what helped me finally adjust.

A very long time before there were mobile phones there were pay phones; phones that hung on the wall and required coins to make a call. There was also the option to make what was called a collect call. The person you were calling had to tell the operator that they would accept the call and would be paying for the charge. So homesick I could hardly stand it, I shuffled down the dorm hallway to the little alcove where the pay phones were.

Dear Dad

You accepted my call and listened to me share my pain. As we talked, you told me I needed to read Psalm 4:8. "In peace I will both lie down and sleep; for you alone, O Lord, make me dwell in safety." That was what I needed to hear that night. Over the next few months, I started to receive cards from you. They were always funny cards and sometimes you would tape a couple of quarters to the inside and tell me to go do some laundry. You knew it cost fifty cents to wash a load of clothes in the dorm. My shame attendant never reminded me about those times when you showed up. He just wanted me to believe that you hadn't loved me.

Thanks for listening, Rachel

I had forgotten about this conversation when in an earlier chapter I said I had never had a meaningful conversation with my dad. I was wrong.

They Will Think

My fear of being laughed at followed me to college. Waiting for my name to be called in speech class made me so nervous my mouth would go dry. The Bible Institute was preparing us to serve in the local church or on the mission field. Knowing how to lead singing was thought to be a good skill to have. After we had spent time during several classes learning how to conduct the different time signatures found in the hymnbook, I sat nervously waiting for my name to be called. It was during those waiting times that I would hear my shame attendant whispering, "They are going to think…" or "They are going to laugh at you." During the days leading up to "show time" it was not unusual to see students walking down the hall conducting an imaginary choir. Every class period I would wonder if this was the day my name would be called. The day arrived and it was my turn. I made my way to the front and was told the page number of the song I was to lead. I had a couple of minutes to practice the right pattern in my head and then I did it. Fortunately, I did not embarrass myself as several students did. But I did have those hours of torture from the shame attendant.

Making More Friends

Meals were served family style. At the beginning of each month our "family" for the month table assignment was posted. Members of the senior class served as the table hosts and hostesses helping to facilitate conversations. Spending a month sharing family style meals twice a day with the same people helped to create friendships. It was during our freshman year that Wayne was assigned to the same table two months in a row and a dating relationship developed with the hostess. More about that later.

I was good at friendship in groups; however, I was not good at dating. My sense of humor worked well in group settings when I was able to just slip in a one liner from time to time. However, the few times that I was asked on a date I didn't know how to relax and just be me. The idea of "date" made me very self-conscious. The first two years I was never asked on a second date.

By the end of the first semester, I had a small group of close friends. Some of the guys had girlfriends back home so they enjoyed the comradery of just being able to hang out together. I was able to just be me. We would gather together in the hallway before meals, sit and visit after dinner, or walk around on campus together. It was during this time that my friendship with Wayne grew. He and a couple of the other guys I was friends with worked in the dish room after meals running the dishwasher and washing pots and pans. I'll let Wayne tell you this story.

Many evenings Rachel would show up and stand at the window and talk to us while we worked. I don't remember how she found out she could make me blush but once she did, she had lots of fun with that information. She would show up at the window and with a big fake southern drawl say, "Hey Wayne, I luv-v-v-v you. I would turn beat red. She had so much fun she would do it all the time. All she had to do was walk up to the window and say, "Hey Wayne," and I would blush.

Not Willing to Risk

School was affordable for everyone because there was no tuition; only room, board, and books. In order to make that possible everyone had a work assignment around campus. We were all required to "volunteer" at least three and a half hours each week. The jobs included waitressing, setting up chairs when the dining hall/classroom/chapel had to be switched, sweeping/shovelling the sidewalks, working in the dish room, working in the Snack Shop, or helping some of the teachers with some of their tasks. Even with no tuition some of the students needed to earn money. Some jobs, like waitressing, would become a paying job after the initial three and a half hours were completed.

Waitressing was one of the jobs that I did not want to do. Each waitress had a group of tables that they set before the meal, then served the food during the meal, and cleaned up after the meal. I did not have a problem with the set up or take down part. It was the walking back and forth to the service window to refill the bowls and platters during the meal that made me not want to be involved. From time to time at the tables where I sat, I had heard jokes made about the waitresses. Putting myself in the position to be the brunt of jokes was not something I was willing to risk.

Music and Travel and Camp

Everyone was enrolled in the Bible/Theology major. I had enrolled with a minor in music. I had no idea what I was signing up for, and it didn't take long for me to figure out that I was not qualified for this program. I did not have the background to do well in music theory and some of the other required courses. (This was the perfect opportunity to hear "Not good enough," from the shame attendant.) I quickly transferred into the Christian Education program.

Even though I wasn't in the music program I was still able to participate in music as a member of the choir. After auditions at the beginning of the semester two groups, Choir and the Ensemble, were formed. I was chosen to be a part of the choir. Most of my close friends had been chosen to be part of the Ensemble. I made new friends in choir, but I really missed my friends when it was time to travel. A couple of weekends a month each group would travel to churches to sing and represent the school. Spring break was choir tour and involved a road trip to sing several concerts during that week. Toward the end of the school year there were auditions to participate in the group that would travel for seven weeks singing in a different church every night except Monday. I became a part of the Gospel Heralds the summer of 1970.

After the tour finished there were still several weeks before school started. Instead of going home I had signed up to be a camp counselor. The camp was part of the school's ministry and many of the campers stayed in the dorm. I had no idea what was involved and found out quickly that I was completely out of my comfort zone. Camping was not going to be my area of ministry.

Camp had already been in session when I joined the staff. Friendships among the counselors had already formed and I wasn't able to become a part of that group. That's the first time I remember feeling like I was on the outside looking in. Wayne was the activities director and on a couple of occasions we spent some time talking together while we waited for the next group of campers to show up on the ball field. (I would learn years later that because of those conversations he had the impression I was more athletic than I really was.) With just three weeks left in the camping season I was tired and so far outside of my comfort zone that I quit and went home. That would not be the last time I quit and went home when I got too far outside of my comfort zone.

Senior Trip

This was a pivotal event in my life with Wayne, so I am going to reminisce with him in this section. Feel free to listen in.

There were four varsities on campus that provided opportunities for us to participate in intramural sports. The only sport that I even considered was soccer because I could play in the backfield and not be the center of attention. While I didn't become center of attention on the field, I did damage my knee and had to be on crutches for a while. Wayne will pick up the story.

Not long after Rachel's injury it was time for our Senior class retreat. We all gathered in the parking lot to decide which car or school van everyone would ride in. Because Rachel was still on crutches and needed to be able to stretch her leg she rode in the middle of the big bench front seat of a 1960s Chevy driven by Paul, one of my good friends. I rode by the window, our class sponsor, and his wife and one other person were in the back. We joined the convoy for the four hour trip to Canton, Ohio.

I didn't know it but as we travelled that first day Rachel was thinking, "Too bad he's taken." I had gotten engaged to the girl I had started dating our freshman year. She had graduated and gone to another school to finish her fourth year and get her degree, so I was part of our "friends" hang out group when I wasn't working at the Dr Pepper plant loading trucks.

I could make up stories about anything and have everyone believing they were true or at least laughing at the silliness of my explanation. I also liked to do the unexpected. I wore "taps" on my shoes that were designed to prevent wear and tear on the heels. Taps also made noise on the concrete floor when we walked down the hall of the main building. I had taps on the shoes I was wearing that day. Suddenly, as we were barrelling down the road at 70 miles an hour, I opened my car door enough to put my foot out and dragged the heel of my shoe with the tap on the pavement so it would make sparks. Paul started yelling, "Wayne, stop that and get your foot back in the car!!!" I just laughed and after a few more sparks pulled my foot back in and continued to laugh as Paul continued to be upset.

A trip to the Football Hall of Fame was on the agenda the next day. As Rachel hobbled along on her crutches I stayed with her. When we got to our next stop, the Canton Baptist Temple, I saw a wheelchair sitting in the lobby and I became her chauffeur for the tour. It was a memorable tour with lots of belly laughs and a few wheelies thrown in for fun.

Back to Campus

We got back to campus and life returned to normal. I rejoined choir that year and travelled some weekends. Many weekends Wayne and his friend Ted and a few other guys would travel to churches and do youth rallies. Life was busy with studies, work, and ministry opportunities. As we were getting close to our Thanksgiving break, Wayne asked me if I would type one of his term papers as I had done in the past. He had two papers that were going to be due shortly after the break and he told me his fiancé would be typing the other one.

The Unexpected Happened

"Hey, can you type my other paper for me?" Wayne asked as soon as he saw me.

"Why, did you have so much fun she didn't have time to get it typed?" I replied.

"No, we broke up." he said.

"Sure, you did," I replied sarcastically. "I'll type your paper," I said, not believing for a minute that they had actually broken up.

As soon as I entered the dorm, I heard the breakup being talked about. It was hard to believe. Several days later I began to notice that everywhere I was, Wayne was there. If I was in the library, he was looking in the window. If I was walking down the steps from the girl's dorm he was at his window in the boy's dorm watching me. Then I noticed that one of his friends would get a goofy, "I know something you don't know," look on his face every time he saw me. It was getting weird. Finally, Wayne asked me to meet him during dating hours. We chatted for a few minutes and then he said, "Do you think there is any chance that we could be more than friends?" It didn't take me long to reply, "As far as I'm concerned, we could be." That was the beginning of our courtship. Wayne told me later that he had purposefully phrased the question that way in case I replied "no" then he could say that he didn't either.

Dating is difficult under the best of circumstances, and we weren't in the best of circumstances. When you've been friends and could talk to each other whenever you wanted, it was strange to become a "couple" and have to follow the dating rules.

During the week we were limited to a couple of hours after dinner. Friday night was the big date night starting with dinner together and ending at nine. Off campus dates had to be double dates and planned and approved ahead of time. Sunday dinner was also a time when couples could spend time together. Since Wayne worked off campus several evenings a week our time was really limited. Despite the limited time we got very serious, very quickly.

During Christmas break he came to Indiana to visit me and "meet the parents." I don't think when he came he had it in your mind that he was going to ask me to marry him but before he left to go back to West Virginia we were engaged. He told me about the conversation he had with my dad when he asked if he could marry me. Dad said, "What do you have to offer Rachel?" Wayne replied, "The Lord's will and a husband that loves her." That ended their conversation. Wow, only one month of actual dating, if you want to call it that, and we were engaged???

Two of the items I found in my treasure box that I mentioned earlier were the presents we had exchanged that first Christmas. I had gotten him an engraved ID bracelet that

I don't think he ever wore. He wasn't really an ID bracelet kind of guy. He got me a little resin statue of a goofy looking little guy all dressed up with a big grin on his face as he looked up at me. Engraved on the side it said, "Get out of my dreams and into my heart." That statue was always part of the décor in my bedroom for years.

The biggest treasure from that time was a notebook that held all of the love notes and cards he had given me while we were in school. Note writing was the big method of connecting between dating couples on campus. The night watchman was the "mailman" between the dorms every night. When he came to the girl's dorm to make sure things were locked up for the night, he would have all the notes the guys were sending, and he would leave with all the notes the girls were sending back. Having kept all those notes and cards helped me remember the sweetness of those days.

My first Valentine card had a really sweet poem in it entitled "If Words Could Match My Love," but the best part was the note he had typed and glued to the back page. It said, *"Rach, The Lord is wonderful. He took my life changed it from one of sin to one of serving Him. He has given me peace that passes my highest expectation of happiness. He has given me the privilege of serving Him for a lifetime. But the most wonderful blessing of all is you. I stand amazed that God has given me the best. Sometimes it seems impossible that in such a short time that I could come to love you so. There are times when I yearn to express my love for you, but there are no words to match my love for you. Because for once in my life I have experienced the love of God through me. My constant prayer is that God will make me a man that is worthy of you. One that will lead as a man, Love as a man, provide as a man, and subject myself unto God as He has ordained. Honey, I long for the day that we would serve Christ together as one, and that day is growing near. How wonderful it is to be in LOVE. All and only yours Wayne.*

What we didn't know was that he was bi-polar. He had manic-depressive illness, the genetic illness that causes extreme mood swings. He had the best laugh, and he loved life when he was manic. He also had a very difficult time with sleep during those manic times. He was never rebellious about the school rules. However, when he couldn't sleep there were times when he would go to one of the classrooms on the other end of the building from the men's dorm with his friend. There was a piano in that room. His friend John would play and they would sing and make cassette tapes for me and John's girlfriend. As far as I know he was never caught.

A paragraph from one of the notes I received while we were dating explains the struggle we both had in our relationship with the Lord while gaining knowledge about Him.

"...I know where the problem lies in spiritual life. I am so hungry for the word that I almost miss where it is. I was really blessed by the word tonight. (This would have been written during our Bible conference right before graduation) I guess when you study textbooks and always in a rush there seems to be no time to study the Word. And man do I need it."

He was so in love with the Lord and passionate about his faith when he arrived at school. Gradually the busyness of study and work stifled some of that passion. He was affected by the rules and expectations that had created my *Good Christian* box. I had been right at home, and my box had stayed intact. Working off campus as much as he did and being able to go home on weekends worked in his favor.

The weekends he didn't go home he and his friends, Ted and Wally, participated in youth rallies. This gave him an outlet to share his faith and kept his passion alive. I had never experienced a passion for Jesus like that. Obedience out of duty does not produce the same passion that comes from obedience out of love and gratitude. He loved Jesus and he was grateful that Jesus had saved him and he wanted to share that with others. Those youth rallies gave him that opportunity and kept him from building his own *Good Christian* box. He had been able to see the school's rules and regulations as how he was expected to live at school. Because those rules and regulations mirrored what I had interpreted as how God expected us to live, my box had stayed intact. Not understanding this difference would become very evident in years to come.

I had romance novel expectations of him that he didn't know about. I wanted life to be like the Valentine card note all the time and would get my feelings hurt easily when it wasn't. One example was the Christmas banquet that happened not long after we started dating. Banquets were not something he enjoyed and he and one of his friends were having fun together instead of him being romantic with me. Wayne asked me later if I was sure it was him that I loved, and not my idea of what I wanted him to be. That was a very astute observation because truthfully, I was afraid if I didn't do everything right he would break up with me. I carried this fear into our marriage. Even though we both wanted to do what God wanted us to do we weren't sure how to figure that out.

Before the semester ended we had an idea that we shared with my parents. Since he had a job, we had a place to live, and my parents were going to be in West Virginia for graduation, we could just get married right after graduation. That idea was not acceptable to my parents and there was no discussion about it. When I talked to a friend about this years later, she suggested that maybe Dad had been afraid about what people would think if I didn't get married in my home church. We continued with plan A.

We were realistic enough to know that there would be problems, but we thought that if we were serving the Lord, we would get through the problem times successfully like my folks had. The wounded bi-polar boy and the wounded naïve girl thought they were ready to face the world together.

So What?

Lord Jesus,

My journal entry from January of 2023 for the last half of this decade read, "You were faithful and good as I lived my legalistic life – longing in my heart for more." I was shocked when I realized how much had happened during that decade from junior high to marriage in ten years. Unpacking those years let me see in a deeper way how Your mercy and grace had been with me all the time.

This is a personalized quote from Dr Thompson, "Those parts of me that feel most broken and that I keep most hidden are the parts that most desperately need to be known by You, so as to be loved and healed." You are omniscient so You already know those broken parts. But it won't be until I understand them and talk to You about them that there will be healing. You knew that this had not yet happened and that I was moving into marriage covered in shame and fear of being exposed. Lord Jesus, You knew I believed that if You and Wayne really knew me neither one of you would love me.

You were still the God Who Sees and You were still my Shepherd so I was not going into this next turbulent time alone.

I Love you, Jesus, more and more all the time. Amen

CHAPTER TEN – READY OR NOT

Graduation and Beyond

Wayne, the first week of May my parents came for graduation and to take me home to plan our wedding. We went to your grandmother's house for a meal right after the ceremony before I headed back to Indiana. We took a walk to say our goodbyes and I wrote my address and phone number on a piece of paper for you. Long distance calls cost between 70 cents and $1.46 a minute depending on what time of day. We weren't expecting to have many phone calls.

I went home and started writing to you every day. Every day I watched for the mailman and every day I was disappointed. It was three weeks before I heard from you. *"Hon,*

I can already read your mind. I bet you are saying, It is about time that idiot wrote me a letter. And this is one time when you would be absolutely right. But believe it or not I have reasons, well would you believe excuses."

You explained in detail what had transpired and ended it with this synopsis, *"I lost your address, I couldn't write until I got it, I couldn't get it until I got your letters, and I didn't get your letters until I got back to Beckley."* What we didn't know was that this behavior of not planning and just doing the next thing without regard for others was part of the bi-polar. I believe with all my heart that God had prepared me to be your wife. Watching my mother take care of my father without complaint was what I knew about being a wife.

I never doubted in all that time that I would eventually get a letter. A few days later I got the second letter. This one didn't have really great news. Our place to live and your job were not going to happen. You were looking for work but it wasn't looking good so you were going to head back to Charleston to your parent's house.

The next letter confirmed that you did not have a job but your dad had given us a car. It never crossed our minds that it might be a good idea to postpone our wedding. One night in June about nine o'clock there was a knock at the door and there you stood. You had borrowed a friend's motorcycle to come see me so we could get our marriage license. Unexpected and unpredictable, that was my man. I was in love and nothing else mattered. We did talk on the phone a few times during those two months apart. I got a total of three letters and we saw each other once.

Here Comes the Bride

My mother was well liked by those outside the family and most people enjoyed being around her. She was very knowledgeable about many things and was willing to share that knowledge with others. She did not have to be emotionally involved to have this type of relationship. But, as I've mentioned, she and I had not bonded, and I was not very kind to my mother those months. I was upset that they hadn't let me stay in West Virginia and get married and my anger and resentment were evident in how I conducted myself.

I didn't include her as I made my plans for my flowers or my cake. Looking back, I'm sure that she was sad and hurt. We did go together to look at wedding dresses after I found one in a magazine that I liked. We went to the store and as I tried it on, she was making mental notes. We then went to the fabric store, found a pattern, bought fabric and the yards and yards of lace. She recreated the dress that I loved. She carefully sewed the yards and yards of lace onto the dress by hand. Not only did she make my dress, but several of the bridesmaid's dresses and all the veils. That had been her showing me love and I didn't recognize it through my immature behavior.

Wayne, the weekend of the wedding finally arrived. My maid of honor, Becky, and one of your groomsmen lived in Ohio and didn't have any way to get to Indiana so you picked them up on your way. Your parents arrived and were staying at a hotel about twenty minutes away from the church. You and John were staying with the family of another one of your groomsmen. They were friends who had lived in West Virginia but now lived about thirty minutes from the church. It was an evening wedding so you decided it would be a good plan to take your two sisters, who were bridesmaids, and two of the groomsmen golfing. By the time you all got back to the house, got showered and changed you were not going to make it to the church in time for pictures. You always said that you weren't late for the wedding because you arrived at the church at precisely 7 p.m. However, there was a lot of miscommunication about meeting places so several of the wedding party were late.

July 21, 1972, northern Indiana was very, very hot. It had never entered my mind when we picked the date for the wedding that it would be brutally hot and that the church was not airconditioned. It was so hot the candles I had put in the candelabras after the rehearsal the night before had melted and were hanging almost upside down when we got to the church that afternoon. I rolled them flat and put them in the refrigerator. Fans filled the windows of the auditorium as they tried to pull the hot air out of the building before the ceremony. It was over 100 degrees in the auditorium when the guests arrived.

The guests were sweltering and the organist kept playing and playing and playing as everyone waited and waited. My family was getting worried but because mom had given me half of a phenobarbital, I was not stressed at all. Everyone arrived, some impromptu pictures were taken of the groom and groomsmen in the basement and the processional was played.

It was about 10 p.m. that night when we finally got back to my house and said our goodbyes to Mom and Dad. Because Becky and John, the maid of honor and the groomsman who you picked up on your way to the wedding had to get back home, they were in the car with us. All my possessions were in the trunk. Becky and all the wedding presents were in the back seat. John and you and I were in the front seat. Mom said that watching me get in the car with someone she had only met three times and leave home for good was one of the hardest things she ever had to do.

The Honeymoon

We stopped to eat sometime during the night. While we waited for our food, you and John went in the backroom and played pool while Becky and I sat at the table. I don't remember ever reading a scene like that in any of my romance novels and my feelings were hurt. We drove on through the night and it was about daylight when we dropped Becky off at home and then drove another hour to John's house. After we dropped him off, we found a motel. They gave us a room that hadn't been cleaned so the maid came in the room with us. By the time she was through cleaning I had fallen asleep. When I woke up you were asleep. We were awakened the next morning when the maid knocked on the door. We packed up and headed for home, which was the attic room over the kitchen at your parents' house. They arrived back home about an hour after we did. That was our honeymoon! We had our personal possessions, our wedding presents, $500.00 in cash, a 1965 Ford Galaxy, no jobs, and no plans.

I woke up early the morning I wrote this section and thought about how incredibly young and unprepared we had been. In my daily devotional e-mail from Scotty Smith, I read these words: "On our wedding day, Darlene and I understood so little about many things, but we were **especially** deficient in our understanding and experience of the truths and riches of the Gospel. We were also naïve and clueless about the wounds, traumas, and brokenness we brought into our marriage. In your perfect timing that changed – boy, did it ever. And your mercy and grace, kindness and love started to be our **oxygen, water, and hope.**"[49] These were just the right words at just the right time. Our wounds, traumas, and brokenness were the perfect environment for the pain that came from unmet expectations to grow as we began our marriage.

Little Wounds – Big Hurts

Wayne, to your mom I was just another one of the kids. She would call for me to come down and help with dinner or anything else she needed. You were right at home and life went on for you. We had taken all of our wedding presents and stored them in the closet in our attic room. In my mind they were our special things to be used someday when we got our own place. For you if you decided something we had could be used right now you would just get it out of the closet and begin using it. Every time that happened I was hurt – little wound – but never said anything.

When we got married, I had not yet learned to drive. You were doing painting and construction jobs at the church next

---

[49] https://www.thegospelxoalition.org/blogs/scotty-smith/53-years-later/

door. I had gone with you in our car to pick up some supplies you needed. When we got back you stopped the car beside the church, got out, and said, "drive the car over to the house." Petrified, I responded, "I've never been behind the wheel of a car before I can't do that." You were insistent and got in the passenger seat and demanded, "Drive the car." I timidly pushed on the gas and inch by inch we circled around to the house and I stopped just short of the carport. "Keep going, I want you to pull under the carport." With my stomach in knots and my hands shaking, without straightening the wheel I pushed on the gas and ran into one of the cinderblock posts that was supporting the carport.

Your family all thought it was funny but I was devastated, humiliated and in tears by the time I got into the house. I went to the refrigerator to put some ice in my glass so I could get a drink only to discover that the ice trays had just been filled so I poured water all over the floor. Again, everyone thought it was funny and tried to make me feel better. That night I would jerk awake time after time as I dreamed about hitting the post. While there was no damage to the car, the carport had to be jacked up in order to realign the post. My self-esteem could not be realigned that easily.

As I had taken on the role of just another kid, I had ceased to be the doting girlfriend/wife you were expecting. At the same time, I had my own unmet expectations to deal with. Where was the young love, newly married romance I had always read about. Those first few months we spent wounding each other without knowing it. That is why when I said, "Wow, we've been married six months," your reply was, "It feels like six years." Not something a young bride wants to hear.

Your former fiancé was beautiful and I was always surprised that you had pursued me. But I had stopped constantly thinking that I was fat. I was full-figured. I had a plump curvaceous body and I had gotten comfortable believing that you loved me just the way I was. I know that you would never have intentionally hurt me in any way. However, you were clueless about how the request you made was going to break my heart. We hadn't been married very long when you asked me if I would go to Weight Watchers. I was stunned. I said, "I thought you loved me just the way I am." As I thought to myself, *Why did you marry me if you didn't like me?* You replied, "I saw you had potential." My shame attendant was right there and immediately I heard him shout, "See, I told you that you weren't good enough." As I wrote those words, I felt the pain and shame of that day. That was a wound that stayed with me the rest of our married life and ultimately led to the writing of this book.

Shame Steals My Joy

In Dr Thompson's book I found these words that perfectly described my feelings. "I assume that before her encounter with the serpent, the woman has lived in a world of anticipated joy. She assumed she was loved and did not need to wonder about it; in the same way she did not need to think about breathing. That is, unless or until something comes along to interrupt it, to shear it off."[50] He explains a few paragraphs later it really doesn't matter if our brain is fully functioning or how shame started in the garden. "What matters is how it is used and how we respond to it when we experience it. Shame is not a mere sensation to be categorized in the same way that we would, say, an itch on my elbow."[51] In the garden it was wielded with intention for the purpose of ruining the world. But that day I was asked to go to Weight Watchers it was wielded by my shame attendant as a way to further destroy my self-image. Dr Thompson reminded me

---

[50] Thompson, The Soul of Shame, 105
[51] Ibid 106

that my emotional distress did not happen without the help of my shame attendant.

Unmet Expectations

Wayne, we had gotten married in July and in October I turned twenty-one. Growing up my birthdays were special. I received my presents at breakfast, and I always had a special dinner and birthday cake. How our families did birthdays was not something we had ever discussed as we dated. There were no presents at breakfast that day. And there was no special dinner or birthday cake. At some point that day your dad did say, "Happy Birthday," but that was the only recognition I got that day. Another unmet expectation and another wound you didn't know happened.

You had gone back to school to get your degree and had gotten a job as a prison guard at a half-way house in the evenings. You shared your faith with one of the men living there. He gave his life to Jesus and got baptized. You mentored him and would go pick him up and bring him to church. You lived your faith every day.

I had gotten a temp job at the Capitol complex that quickly became permanent. Our 1965 Ford was starting to give us problems so we did what any young, dumb couple would do, we bought a new car. We had gone car shopping and I assumed when it was time to go get the car we would do it together, after all it was going to be our car. I was very wrong. I rode to and from work with your dad and one day when we got home there was our new car. Everyone in the family had already been for a ride before I ever saw it and another romance novel dream was crushed.

I was not the only one experiencing unmet expectations. We didn't have any pets when I was growing up so had no experience taking care of them. Your family had a dog and Donna had a duck named Gertrude. The weekend the rest of the family was away we were in charge of the pets. While we were getting ready for church that Sunday evening you wanted me to go feed Gertrude who was down in the little shed at the back of the property near the river. You had no idea I was afraid to go down there and were not happy when I wouldn't do it. It turned into our first big fight. You couldn't understand why I wouldn't do what you asked and I didn't know how to explain why I couldn't. More pain inflicted on the walking wounded.

Things weren't going well and one Sunday night I went up front at the end of the church service and prayed with someone. You had enough of your own unmet expectations about what marriage should look like that later you told me, "I was planning to leave that night, and if I had left, I would never have come back." We never discussed it again but I never forgot what you said. It was always in the back of my mind that you could leave.

That's enough stories. We had no clue that we were wounding each other as we tried to figure out this thing called marriage. Once my job had become permanent, we found a little mobile home several miles from your parents. It was probably one of the first ones ever built and it was so far up the "holler" that the sun didn't get over the mountain until about ten in the morning and went down on the other side about four in the afternoon. As my dad liked to say, "You're so far up there that they have to pump daylight to you." We had no phone and many days all we did was go there to sleep but we had our own place.

So What?

Lord Jesus,

What can I say? It's only by Your grace that we survived those days. The baggage we both brought into our marriage would fill a small storage unit. My wounds bumped his

127

wounds and his wounds bumped mine. You had plans for us and Your grace and mercy kept us together as You were preparing us for our next step. You weren't judging us because we didn't have it all together. This was definitely a time when You were our Good Shepherd. We were failing, stumbling, and losing our way but You knew our hearts and You kept calling us to follow You. Wayne's love for You showed in everything he did. I still had so much growing to do. You still saw my heart even when my shame attendant wanted me to think I wasn't getting it right. He wanted me to think I should be running when I had barely learned to walk and all the time You were loving me. It would be a long time before I found the verse in Zephaniah 3:17 that told me that you take great delight in me, quiet me with Your love and rejoice over me with singing. My word picture for that verse has always been a mother pulling her child onto her lap when they need comfort. After a time of loving and comfort the mother sets the child down and with a little pat tells them to go play. You don't ever set me down reminding me of the depth of Your love for me.

Something else I've been learning that refutes the lies that I didn't have it right and I wasn't good enough, comes from my time spent memorizing Romans chapter 8. In that chapter I learned that when I didn't know how to pray the Holy Spirit was praying for me according to Your will. Thank you that You led me, guided me, carried me, disciplined me, and loved me then and now.

More in love than ever before,
Rachel

CHAPTER ELEVEN – THE U-HAUL YEARS PART ONE

"For my thoughts are not your thoughts, neither are your ways my ways."
Isaiah 55:8-9 (NIV)

What You Don't Know...

The rest of that statement says, "can't hurt you." What a total lie. What Wayne and I didn't know about each other led to many hurts. We didn't know that when I had been molested as a child my four-year-old mind had determined it wasn't safe to trust anyone and had locked up emotionally. We didn't know that my *Good Christian* box gave me the illusion that I was in control. Wayne had no way to know that I believed the lie that I wasn't enough and that his request for me to go to Weight Watchers confirmed that lie and pushed on that wound. I didn't know that he was trying to be affirming when he said, "I saw you had potential." We didn't know that he was undiagnosed bi-polar. I didn't know that those times when he "crashed" and couldn't get out of bed it wasn't that he didn't want to, it was because the depression was overwhelming. I didn't know that those times caused him great pain internally because he knew what he was capable of but he was unable to perform. We didn't understand that our Heavenly Father had been fully aware of everything we didn't know and that He had good plans for us. We didn't have any understanding about the role suffering was designed to play in our spiritual growth. We knew we loved the Lord and we wanted to do His will the best way we knew how. However, we didn't really *KNOW* this God we were trusting any more than we *KNEW* each other but we were going to learn about both through the good, the bad, and the hard times.

U-Haul Stop Number One

In February of 1973, seven months after we got married, Wayne got a call from his former roommate who was pastoring a church in Tennessee. The church had been growing rapidly and they were looking for a youth pastor. We were asked to come and visit and see if we would be a good fit. After the visit the church asked us to come. Our compensation package was $25.00 a week and we would live in the basement of the parsonage. We accepted their offer, packed up our meager belongings, and headed into our first official ministry opportunity carrying our wounds, traumas, and brokenness with us.

As I looked back over the time we spent in Tennessee, that voice inside my head wanted me to have regrets and to be filled with "if only" thoughts. However, what God wanted me to hear was the truth from Proverbs 16:9, "A person's heart plans his way, but the LORD determines his steps." When I reviewed the twenty-two months we ministered there through that lens, it was healing.

The church had been growing rapidly in part because of their bus ministry. As a result, a Sunday school addition was under construction when we arrived. Wayne was the youth pastor and was part of the construction crew; he had also acquired a bus route. Old school buses need repair so he was also the bus mechanic. This was exactly what he needed. He was happiest and most productive when he had plenty of manual labor to keep him occupied. He loved the kids in the youth group and they loved him. He was athletic, charismatic and he loved Jesus. The church was blessed by his ministry.

Taking Care of Wayne

When I looked at what my part of the ministry had been it was easy for me to believe the lie that I hadn't really contributed anything. The day we arrived we had been shown our new living quarters. The basement, including the bathroom, was entirely covered with green indoor outdoor carpeting. It had not been designed as a place for someone to live permanently.

Saturday mornings our kitchen was used for the bus ministry breakfast. The youth group went through our living space to get to the part of the basement where they met. I had to coordinate with the pastor's wife so I could use their laundry room to wash our clothes. That basement never felt like a home to me.

My first job was at the shirt factory and I later switched to the boot factory because they paid better. Occasionally I played the piano for church and I took care of Wayne. That last part – took care of Wayne – that was my most important job. I was able to do that job because I had learned from my mother what it meant to serve my husband. I provided the stability that was so hard for him. One of the notes Wayne had written to me when we first started dating confirmed this.

"Thanks, honey, for all your love. I had never needed anyone, but now I know that I need you. *I need your love to comfort me, your touch to reassure me, and your laughter to make me happy. I need you Rach; to make my life complete to allow me to sufficiently fulfil the commands that the Lord has given us. I can think of no greater pleasure than that of spending my life loving you, sharing with you, and providing for you. You have, in our short time together become a part of me. An unmoveable part."*

Love, Wayne

Of course, as newlyweds and just because we were human we bumped each other's wounds. My shame attendant latched onto one and it stayed an open wound for many years. It was our first anniversary and we didn't have much money. Wayne and the pastor had Monday's off and had started golfing every week. They got to the course at daylight and stayed until dark. We decided we would use the money we had to get Wayne a set of golf clubs as his anniversary present. We drove to Nashville to buy the clubs. Something I said on the way home upset him enough that he pulled off the road, got out of the car, and sat on the back bumper for a few minutes. When he had finally gotten back in the car he said, "You have never seen me lose my temper, and by the grace of God you never will, but if you do you will never forget it."

He then told me about the time he got in a fight back in junior high. He said,

"I was so angry I was beating the boy to the point someone had to pull me off before I really hurt him. When I realized what I could have done I locked down that anger and I didn't ever want it to come out again."

He was telling me that he didn't want to lose his temper and hurt me. What I heard was that it was my responsibility to never make him mad.

I Should Already Know

Christmas had come and I found out that the pastor and his wife were going to be taking vacation over the holidays. She had been in charge of the Christmas program the year before and by default it was now my turn. I hadn't been asked if I wanted to be in charge. It had just been assumed that not only would I but that I had the skills to do it. After all I had been to Bible School and I had a diploma in Christian

Education so "I should already know" how to direct a Christmas program.

I hadn't questioned it. I had tried to figure out how to make it happen because if "I should already know how" it hadn't been ok to ask for help. I had never been involved at any level with a Christmas program but I had heard about the one from the previous year. There had been rehearsals which required the buses to pick up the kids and bring them to the church on Saturday. I hadn't wanted to ask for that kind of help. Long story short, the Christmas program that year was polar opposite to the one from the year before. There had been no extra rehearsals and no elaborate costumes. Even though no one ever said it, I believed that everyone thought it had been a failure. The healing part of that memory came when I realized that the purpose of the Christmas program had been to tell the story of Jesus' birth and that had happened. It had not been a failure. It had just been different and another lie was exposed.

What We Did Mattered

As I had begun work on this chapter, I found myself thinking about one of the teenagers that had been in this youth group. I thought, *I wish I could talk to John.* Less than a month later I was on a trip and realized I was only an hour away from where he lived. I contacted him and was able to spend an afternoon with him and his wife.

Spending that time with John answered any questions I had about the impact of our ministry. As we talked, he shared that he had been in an extremely rebellious phase when we arrived. Because of Wayne's experiences as a teenager, he had been able to relate to John and they had connected. God used Wayne as he shared his testimony of God's grace in his life. He also used his example of hard work and love for the Lord to help John as well. It hadn't been long before he surrendered his life to God's leading and had begun to actively pursue his relationship with the Lord.

One of his favorite memories had been about all the time that we spent with him and two of his friends every Wednesday night after youth group was over. We met in our basement where there was a piano. I would play the piano and the guys would pick out song after song from the hymnbook. This would go on until my fingers were worn out and I couldn't play another song. (It didn't matter that my sister's ability came naturally, the ability I had worked hard for had been used.)

I don't remember what I did with my spare time during the time we were there. I only had one friend. The culture of that small town was not conducive to developing friendships with outsiders. It had been such a lonely time for me and I hadn't been able to see how anything I had done had been worthwhile. The visit with John had exposed that lie. What I had done to take care of Wayne had been seen. My contribution had been remembered. John's mother had been my one friend and she had often talked about the influence I had there. What we had done there, in our young inexperienced way, was still bearing fruit.

Looking back, I saw one thing that had been missing for Wayne. He didn't have a mentor in his life. He hadn't been in the pastoral studies at school. He didn't have any of the training that those planning to go into the pastorate had experienced. My loneliness had become more apparent to both of us. By this time the building addition had been completed and his workload was drastically reduced. We were both feeling the need for a change.

All of my old lies were still there – I needed to be perfect, I should already know, I'm here for others, and God is disappointed with me. And I had added that I was also responsible for Wayne's emotions.

U-Haul Stop Number Two

In May of 1974 we got a call from a church in Virginia about a possible youth pastor position. I still remember that we sat on the porch in front of the church and talked about what we should do. This time our compensation package was $70.00 month and they would pay our rent. Wayne would also work as the manager of the Christian Bookstore in town. After we considered everything, we decided that if they asked us to come, we would accept. They asked – we accepted. May of 1974, we loaded the U-Haul once again, left Tennessee and moved to Virginia leaving our health insurance behind not knowing that I was pregnant. My first pregnancy test at the OBGYN in Virginia was negative. We were disappointed but figured that was for the best. When I had a follow up appointment and a second pregnancy test, it was positive. I soon started dealing with significant morning sickness so finding a job wasn't easy. There is a saying that wherever you go there you are and that was true. All our unresolved traumas, wounds, brokenness, and Wayne's bi-polar were right there with us. We were headed for some really turbulent times over the next year and a half.

To Steal Kill and Destroy

I Peter 5:8, "Be sober-minded; be watchful. Your adversary the devil prowls around like a roaring lion, seeking someone to devour." – Actively seeking to harm and devour, much like a hungry lion seeking prey. He was definitely prowling around in Virginia when we got there.

Ephesians 4:27, "give no opportunity to the devil" – Things were going to happen that gave him every opportunity to wreak havoc in our lives.

Romans 8: 38-39, "For I am persuaded that neither death nor life, nor angels nor rulers, nor things present nor things to come, nor powers, nor any other created thing will be able to separate us from the love of God in Christ Jesus our Lord." In the middle of all the chaos God was there and we were never out of his care.

I Corinthians 10:4-5, "The weapons we fight with are not the weapons of the world. On the contrary, they have divine power to demolish strongholds. We demolish arguments and every pretension that sets itself up against the knowledge of God, and we take captive every thought to make it obedient to Christ."

We didn't know how to use these weapons and the power of the Holy Spirit and there were some strongholds erected in our lives. We didn't understand that the battle we were fighting, we weren't going to be able to win on our own. We lost a lot of battles but thankfully the war had already been won for us by Christ on the cross. And now, our lost battles can be redeemed as others learn from our mistakes.

The only thing that lets me share this next section is that I know that God never, never, ever, stopped loving either one of us. He was not disappointed in us. We did grieve him. We engaged in behaviors that were contrary to God's will and character causing the Holy Spirit to sorrow but not to stop loving us.

A passage from my *The Soul of Shame* book sets the stage for these next pages. "Shame is not something we "fix" in the privacy of our mental processes; evil would love for us to believe that to be so. We combat it within the context of conversation, prayer, and other communal, embodied actions." [52]

As I look back over our lives that is something we never had or did. Neither one of us had that needed "older" person in our life. That person who held us accountable, asked us how things were going and prayed with us. We didn't have

---

[52] Thompson, The Soul of Shame, 17-18

community where we could be vulnerable. We kept our shame to ourselves and therefore we never were able to truly address it.

The one constant in the stories told in *The Soul of Shame* was that healing didn't come without vulnerability. *Redeeming Shame in Our Nurturing Communities* is the title of Chapter eight in that book. As I wrote this book I was surrounded by community. It had already been redeeming for me and for those who have been with me on this journey before it was ever published. It was with much trepidation that I wrote about our struggles. My shame attendant shouted long and loud about what people would think about us if I shared. However, after much prayer I concluded that Wayne would want me to share this part of our story. I looked at all the poems he had written years later and found this one that says it all as he referenced the struggle Paul describes in Romans 7:14-25 in the third stanza.

IN CHRIST THERE IS FORGIVENESS OF SIN

We struggle through this life day after day.
Our mistakes can be counted by the score.
But Christ is the forgiver of sin.
And we can trust his forgiveness ever more.

Sin can creep upon us unaware.
It causes us from God to stray.
But upon the confession of our sin
Jesus can take our sin away.

Paul said it best in the Word.
The things that I would not I do
The things that I would I do not
But sin is forgiven it's true.

As far as the east is from the west.
Into the depths of the deepest sea
That is how far Christ took my sins.
And now from these agonies I am free.

Wayne,

One story I remember you telling me was about the time your dad set you down to have "The Talk." Your response was, "Yeah, Dad, what do you want to know." He got up and left the room. You had been introduced to sex in the janitor's closet at school in the sixth grade by an older girl. If I remember correctly there were also pornographic materials in your life later. Before you came to faith you were also sexually active with some of your girlfriends.

Fast forward to you and me. I was as naïve as they came. We obeyed the dating rules when we were at school. I couldn't sign out to go to your house for the weekend but I could sign out to go to a girlfriend's house. Once at her house her mother would give me permission to go stay at your house. We did not discuss and/or set in place any boundaries about physical contact.

During one of my pastor's sermons, he talked about walking in light from Ephesians 5:3 "But do not let immorality or any impurity or greed even be named among you..." He went on to explain that the word there for immorality in the original language is porneia. He defined it this way, "any sexual expression outside of a husband and wife in marriage." It's easy to read those verses in our language and gloss over them when you don't have a complete understanding of what the word immorality means. However, based on this definition our behavior while we were dating would qualify as immoral. During that time my conscience and my shame attendant had made sure to let me know that I had been sinning. My fear of losing you had been greater than my desire to trust God with the outcome if I said no to the intimacy we expressed. There always had been a sense of pride that at least we didn't "go all the way." Fortunately, our courtship was short and we were away from each other for a lot of it or we might not have been able to say that.

*This brings me back to our time in Virginia. We never discussed our pre-marital physical relationship. In fact, we never discussed a lot of things about life. I had reached my Weight Watcher goal not long before I got pregnant. I was seven months pregnant when you brought the first magazine home. My shame attendant was right there any time the magazines appeared telling me this was about me being "not good enough." I have been learning about sexual addiction, as well as the sexual component that can be part of bi-polar and I'm able to know that this was **your** problem. My heart is still catching up to that and I'm healing. Access to*

139

pornography was much more limited in the 70's and it definitely wasn't ever discussed at church. However, it was there.

Wayne, you would not believe all the ugliness that is accessible to men and women alike and how early boys and girls are being exposed. This was going to be an ongoing struggle throughout our marriage. I Corinthians 10:13 says it all, "No temptation has overtaken you that is not common to man. God is faithful, and he will not let you be tempted beyond your ability, but with the temptation he will also provide the way of escape, that you may be able to endure it." There are so many resources available now that weren't available then which could have provided that way of escape.

It has taken writing this book for me to understand that while this caused untold harm to me and to you it was one of the weapons the evil one used to try to kill our relationship, steal our joy, and destroy our lives. As time marched on, we were growing in our relationship with the Lord and at the same time there was a stronghold running parallel.

As I already said, Jesus had already paid the price for our sin and he knew the struggle we had and loved us completely. Psalm 103:8 "The Lord is merciful and gracious, slow to anger, and plenteous in mercy." He showed us much mercy over those years.

God gave me two Godly men who had also experienced your struggle that helped me understand, as much as a woman can understand a man, how hard this was for you as well. Healing slowly happened for me and you are already healed and enjoying heaven.

School of Hard Knocks

The pastor of the church that asked us to come had known he was going to be resigning not long after we got there but hadn't told us. It was a surprise to us and it wounded Wayne.

We weathered that storm and he continued building his relationships with the youth.

What happened next really rocked him. A new pastor came and things didn't go well. We chose not to participate in a multi-level marketing venture with him and his wife and he wasn't happy about that. I would learn later how poorly he treated Wayne after that. Wayne maintained his integrity and continued to work at the bookstore and serve as youth pastor. But he was wounded once again.

February 1975 on my due date Wayne was so sick we took him to the doctor's office. We didn't understand until many years later that he was experiencing a major manic episode. While we were waiting to see the doctor, he was so agitated he couldn't sit still. There was a hallway in the doctor's office that went completely around the inside of the building. He was in that hallway running as fast as he could around and around until the doctor could see him. He sent us directly to the hospital. I still remember that they brought me the wheelchair thinking I was there to deliver.

The doctor had promised that they would give him something to help his agitation once he got settled in. Wayne told me later that he called the doctor from his room in the middle of the night because he was still so agitated. The doctor told him that he couldn't believe that with everything they had already given him it hadn't helped. They kept him for several days but we left with no real diagnosis.

Just a few days later Nathan Wayne Stewart joined our family. Wayne was in love. I always say that I birthed Nathan and his dad took him. As a result, Nathan and I never established the joyful securely attached relationship Dr Thompson talked about. He was a bottle baby so Wayne would call and ask if I had fed him yet. If I said no, he wanted me to wait so he could feed him. Nathan went with Wayne everywhere he could possibly take him. This was before car seats so as soon as Nathan could sit up, he rode in the car with his dad sitting on his left leg.

We moved four times during the months we lived there. The first place we lived didn't allow children. We had been in the process of packing to move when Wayne got sick so at nine months pregnant with the help of some men from the church, I got us moved.

Wayne, May of 1975 was a tough month. You had taken the youth group to camp and I had stayed home with Nathan. I got a phone call that your grandfather had died so I went to the camp and found you to let you know. At that point we didn't know what had happened. You would find out that he had committed suicide. You were very close to him and it was very difficult.

To make it even more challenging we left from his funeral to drive to Indiana for my sister's wedding. I was not at all cognizant of your pain and I got caught up in the wedding. The more I understand about childhood trauma and emotions the more I can forgive myself for not being as compassionate as I would like to have been. At the same time your emotions were locked up too. It's hard to hug each other when your arms are crossed protecting yourself.

Later that month you were ordained. Your sister was getting married and she wanted you to perform her ceremony and you had to be ordained to be licensed in West Virginia. In June we went back to West Virginia and you performed the wedding for Donna and Bruce.

Not long after that things changed at the church and we decided we couldn't stay there any longer. We now had to pay our own rent and the job at the Christian Bookstore had stopped. Wayne got a job working as a cook at a Denny's. After Nate was born, I started working at a garment factory. One of our friends got Wayne a job at the furniture factory. He excelled there just like he excelled every place he worked.

The third move we made took us closer to his work and with rent we could afford.

No matter where he was or what he was doing he cared about the people around him. He met a young man at the factory that he befriended and when we moved once again to a little house David came to live with us. Even though Wayne was being wounded by those who should have been mentoring him it didn't stop him from mentoring and ministering to others.

We became part of a small start-up church and Wayne volunteered to serve as the youth pastor. We received a small stipend. When a church in Indiana asked us to come the little church offered more money for us to stay. Wayne felt that if he was worth more money when he said he was leaving he should have been worth that while we were there. We didn't accept their offer to stay.

So What?

Heavenly Father,

When I dig through the first half of this decade my shame attendant wants me to hear and believe there were so many things I "should have known." He doesn't want me to understand what your name, Jehovah-mekoddishkem – The God Who Sanctifies, means. He doesn't want me to understand that the sanctification process started the day Wayne and I surrendered our lives to you. Now I see the things that happened to us during that time of our life were part of our sanctification process. I couldn't see any spiritual growth happening any more than I could see my feet growing when I was a child. Growth physically and spiritually is a gradual process. So, I'm going to keep digging and keep finding You more and more.

Thanks for walking with me on this journey,
Rachel

CHAPTER TWELVE – THE U-HAUL YEARS PART TWO

When I am afraid, I will trust in you.
Psalm 56:3

Here We Go Again

This move took us to my home church in Northern Indiana. My dad had been the pastor but had retired because of his Parkinson's disease. When we arrived, they didn't have a new pastor yet. Wayne was bi-vocational and worked with my brother as an auto mechanic. His hours were such that it was hard to spend as much time as he would have liked with the young people.

I got a job at the hospital as a ward clerk and worked midnights. Nate had some adjustment issues until we found the right childcare for him. He was a fun toddler and he and his dad were joined at the hip. He even had some little overalls that had a service station patch on it just like his dad's work shirts.

Wayne had been very open about his style as a youth pastor when he interviewed and thought everyone was on the same page. However, as time went on his methods started to be questioned. There were a couple of very hurtful incidents involving gossip that really wounded Wayne. This would have been a time when having an older man in his life would have helped him get healing for his wounds. Instead, he just kept on doing what he thought God wanted him to do and stuffed the hurts.

I would describe my life during that time as being on auto pilot. I was back home and my *Good Christian* box was firmly intact. I'd had years of practice at coloring inside the lines and I was very much aware of everything I did because I didn't want anyone to think anything bad about me.

After one particularly deep wounding, we got a call from Wayne's former youth leader in West Virginia. He was now the director of a Christian Children's Home that was part of the Union Gospel Mission. He asked us to come as residential childcare workers at the home. Wayne would also serve as the Chaplain. So once again we loaded up the truck. We had been in Indiana for eighteen months. There was a pattern here that would make sense later.

West Virginia Here We Come

We became house parents for the junior high boys at Brookside Children's Home in Charleston, West Virginia. We quickly found our roles and made a great team. The facility had a pool and a gym. There was also an activities director and he and Wayne became great friends. Wayne was once again thriving with a new cause and lots of physical activity.

He led chapel services on Sunday and had devotions at mealtime. He was well liked and respected by the boys. He always liked to think outside the box and even though he would get approval for some of his ideas from our superiors, our peers didn't always buy in. This caused some friction. We didn't know for a long time that before he called us, the Director had already offered our position to another couple. But when he found out that we were thinking about moving back to West Virginia he offered it to us. When we accepted, he rescinded their offer. That was bad all by itself, but then we found out that the couple to whom he offered it were relatives of the high school boys' house parents who lived on the other end of the dorm. No wonder they hadn't welcomed us with open arms.

Many years later I found this letter Wayne had written during our time at Brookside.

Lord,

I have often wondered why Paul would fear being a castaway. He being a man that was seemingly faultless, writing the better part of the New Testament. A man that stood before King Agrippa fearlessly, who was shipwrecked, snake bitten, stranded at sea, and still his only concern was to preach Christ.

Now, after being saved for almost ten years, I am beginning to feel the same pressure that Paul must have felt. Pressure of consistency, saying the right things, going the right places, having the right answers, the right actions, and the right reactions. The pressure of supplying spiritual help to others until he seem drained himself. The pressure of giving over every minute to the desires of the Spirit rather than his own desires.

I now realize that being willing to share, to work, to witness, to preach and to pray are the easier parts of the ministry. The harder part is to keep me in the relationship with Christ so that I have something fresh and real to share and teach to others. To deflate my selfish desires, goals, and dreams, and to replace those with the leading of the Spirit.

Lord, I wanted you to know that the lesson you have been teaching is comprehended. Not that I will never fail but at least I know that I have the same power that Paul had. The power of the Holy Spirit.

Thank you, Lord, for not quitting on me.

Wayne

This was just another example of a time it would have been good for Wayne to have had a mentor. My shame attendant wanted me to hear, "You should have known." He wanted me to believe I had failed because I had no idea what was going on in Wayne's head. I didn't listen to that voice, instead I realized that we were a very good team, each taking care of our own responsibilities, and looking out for each other. However, we were both so wounded and locked up emotionally that we weren't connected emotionally. That made me sad.

It couldn't have been long after he wrote his letter to God that he had an idea for helping the boys. He wanted to use the property we owned down in the country to take the boys camping and teach them how to do some construction projects. The Mission had lots of materials lying around that could be used for those purposes. It wasn't long before he heard it suggested that he just wanted to get a cabin built on our property. That wound was the last straw. We didn't know that this event coincided with what turned out to be his first full blown bi-polar depression.

We had been at the Child Care Center for not quite two years when he was DONE! Done with that job and done with church ministry. What he was really done with was the *"What A Good Christian Looks Like"* box. He had been hurt for the last time by those who claimed to be "Good Christians." He had never gotten in the box but he was being judged unjustly by those who were. I didn't know that he was done with church in general, not just ministry. I believed once we got settled and found a church, things would be okay.

On January 1, 1980, we packed the U-Haul one more time and headed to Kentucky.

City Girl in the Woods

Wayne, the memories you had of your time in Kentucky as a kid made you think of it as a safe place with safe people. Your best friend, Bobby, was one of those safe people. You called him and he gave you a job driving a lumber truck and let us move into his A-frame hunting cabin in the woods. Your city girl really struggled with that move. Your dad helped us move and when we finally got to the road where the cabin was, we discovered that there was no way to get the U-Haul up to the cabin. We had to off load our things onto our little 4x4 Chevy Luv truck one load at a time and slowly get it up the road. We found that there was no electricity, no water, and no phone. When everything was safely in the house, Nathan and I got back in the U-Haul with your Dad and headed back to West Virginia. Once you got things cleaned up and the electricity turned on you came and got us. I had always jokingly said, "I'll live with you anywhere as long as there is running water and it isn't me running for it." However, this time there was still no water and I did have to run to the creek and carry water. The cabin was only five miles from town but with the condition of the coal truck roads it would take almost an hour to get there.

Once Nathan and I came back, you started your job. We would ride into town everyday with you so I could look for work. We would drop you off at the lumber yard and go to Bobby's mom's house and spend the day. Bettye became a dear friend and lifeline during that time.

You started having stomach problems and were diagnosed with Irritable Bowel Syndrome. The doctor suggested that you needed to add some physical activity to your life. You joined the city softball team and the first game, first inning, you slide in home and broke your ankle. Your job was gone and you were now staying in the woods by yourself every day. This was not healthy at all. You started doing everything you had done before you had become a believer. You started smoking again and drinking to the point that I was afraid you were becoming an alcoholic. All of these things were your way of trying to numb your pain. You really believed that God had let you down. With our 20/20 hindsight we know that this was your first "major" depression of our married life. I have also learned that it isn't unusual for a person suffering with this illness to have a crisis of faith like this. I know the struggle it is for me to deal with the shame attendant and I didn't have a mental health issue so I can't begin to imagine what it was like for you.

Your crisis of faith became mine as well. I had never had to live my faith alone. I had depended on my family and then on you and hadn't been put to the test. I didn't know what to do when push came to shove and the walls of my *Good Christian* box got tested. I didn't know what I would do or where I would go without you. I truly loved you with all my heart so I tried to follow you for a while. I wanted you to be happy. For the first time in my life, I tasted liquor and I quit going to church too. That was a true change in thinking for me. We lived so far from town and I didn't know anyone so it was just easier to quit going to church.

That didn't last long because I missed the fellowship of other believers and didn't enjoy the choices I was making. I tried one church that I decided you would go to with me if you started back. I was desperately praying for you to find your way back to God. It didn't take me long to discover that I had not found the right church. My new friend Betty loved the Lord so I started going to church with her. I joined the choir and before long I found myself leading the ladies Sunday School class but I still hadn't found my way to being in God's Word daily. However, I was starting to figure out what I truly believed about my faith and not just what I had been taught to believe. This was going to take a long time.

Being around ladies who loved Jesus but weren't confined to the *Good Christian* box was new for me.

Those two years in Kentucky were the beginning of me trying to serve two masters. Fortunately, God knew my heart. He knew that I really wanted to please Him. He also knew that I had been raised to do whatever it took to please you. When I was trying to please you, I believed that God wasn't happy with me. I put on my best spiritual face and spent those years knowing that when I was following what God wanted, you weren't happy with me. But if I tried to do what God wanted, I could lose our marriage. Divorce had been like a four-letter word in my house growing up. I believed that if I got divorced, I would disgrace the entire family and be a total spiritual failure. I had also been taught that if you divorced, you could never remarry. I was only 29 years old and had a four-year-old son. What would I do? When I was following you, I was covered in shame. One of the hallmarks of healing is being vulnerable enough to share your shame and allow God's truth to heal you. No one can do that alone. It is scary and it is hard. The shame attendant didn't want to let me go and SCREAMED– "WHAT WILL PEOPLE THINK?" if you expose your struggle.

Wayne, remembering those days was very heavy for me. Reviewing the struggle and the choices I made during that time left me feeling condemned. Just what my shame attendant wanted. I went to bed burdened and crying out to God that night. I told him I didn't know where to go from here and that He would have to help me know what to say next. When I woke up at 3:30 the next morning one of the verses I had been memorizing from Romans chapter eight came rushing back to me. "There is therefore no condemnation for those who are in Christ Jesus." God wasn't condemning you or me for what we had done. He had already taken the punishment for all of our sins, past, present, and future.

Paul understood exactly what we had been experiencing during that time in our lives. Paul explained our conundrum in Romans 7:18-21 when he says, "For I know that nothing good dwells in me, that is, in my flesh. For I have the desire to do what is right, but not the ability to carry it out. For I do not do the good I want, but the evil I do not want is what I keep on doing. Now if I do what I do not want, it is no longer I who do it, but sin that dwells within me."

What did that mean when he said it wasn't him but the sin that dwelt in him? I pondered that question for quite a while. Then I asked my pastor how he would explain it. He said that he believed that Paul was so broken by his past and his sin that he saw himself personified as sin. That he was his sin. But he came to understand that his sin nature was still a part of him. Paul explains this in verses 21-28. "So, I find it to be a law when I want to do right, evil lies close at hand. For I delight in the law of God, in my inner being, but I see in my members another law waging war against the law of my mind and making me captive to the law of sin that dwells in my members. Wretched man that I am! Who will deliver me from this body of death? Thanks be to God through Jesus Christ our Lord! So then, I myself serve the law of God with my mind, but with my flesh I serve the law of sin."

It is at this point that Paul made his declaration in Romans 8:1, "There is therefore no condemnation for those who are in Christ Jesus." As I remembered all of this, I felt the shame fall away. This didn't mean there hadn't been need for repentance. It just meant we were still God's children who needed to grow in grace and in the knowledge of God. It meant that sanctification was a life-long process. Philippians 1:6 came to mind, "And I am sure of this, that he who began a good work in you will bring it to completion at the day of Jesus Christ."

Wayne, we were young and dumb. There was so much we didn't know. Just because we had gone to Bible school and passed the classes didn't mean we had absorbed all the knowledge. We were trying to do calculus without a strong foundation in algebra, geometry, trigonometry, and pre-calculus. Were we still sinning? YES!! Was God grieved by our sin? YES! Was he disappointed in us? NO! Because to be disappointed someone has to have failed to fulfil your hopes or expectations. God knew what we were going so we did not fail to fulfil any of his expectations. God's love for us never wavered and our struggles were going to make us stronger.

However, we weren't there yet. We still had a long road ahead of us. I grew so weary of the struggle. We had never recovered financially from your time off work with your broken leg. We had moved into town and Nathan had started Kindergarten. I found a job at an insurance agency. Your cast was finally off, and you could start to look for work too. Your depression still had a grip on you, and I had to convince you that you could take a job cleaning up used cars at the Ford dealership. You took that job and quickly advanced to assistant service manager, but we still weren't getting out of the hole financially or spiritually.

Trying to Find Help

I didn't have any idea the depth of your spiritual struggle. You and my brother, Tim, had always gotten along well and I reasoned that if you were able to spend time with him that you would change back to the man I had married, hoping I could get back in my comfort zone. I was so tired of the constant struggle. What I didn't recognize in my quest to obey the rules was that you were the man I married. You were a kind and compassionate man, who always saw the good in other people, and you were always willing to help. You were much better at being an example of Christ to others than I was. As I looked back over those years and saw how emotionally locked up I had been it was very clear that my compassion level was on empty. I didn't understand how much you were suffering or know how to help alleviate your pain.

Back in the U-Haul

Wayne, we did move to Indiana; there was the potential for a job that was going to help us get our finances in order. You and Nathan were absolutely miserable. We moved Nathan in the middle of second grade. Every morning, I would send him out with his cousins to get on the bus and not long after the bus left the doorbell would ring and there he would be. He had intentionally missed the bus. I would load him in the car and take him to school. He was the little Kentucky boy having to fit into a whole different culture. When we moved into our own place, he did a bit better in the new school which was a bit more inner city.

Our marriage took a big hit. I was back home, I had jumped right back into my *Good Christian* box, and I know you felt judged by me and others. You lasted a year and though we still loved each other we decided to separate and you thought we should divorce. It didn't seem that we would be able to work out our differences and all three of us were miserable. Finances hadn't changed either and we filed for bankruptcy. One of the worst days of my life was January 1, 1983, when you and Nathan left Indiana. You told me that as you pulled out of the driveway Nathan threw up his hands like a touchdown and said, "Whoopee, I can't wait to get out of this place." You went to live with your mom and dad in West Virginia. I stayed in Indiana and moved back into my brother's house in the basement where my parents lived. We had been married for eleven and a half years.

I reached out to a pastor friend who lived nearby and went to talk to him. He gave me one piece of advice I always remembered. He said, "Just remember Rachel, the final chapter has not been written yet." He was so right.

You came to Indiana to visit so we could go to bankruptcy court. You had a list of questions for both of us to answer and then we compared our answers. On paper, we had what appeared to be significant irreconcilable differences. You went back to West Virginia, and I made plans to take vacation time and come get Nathan and go see our friends in Kentucky.

The day I arrived and pulled in you met me in driveway and handed me a letter then went back inside. I stayed out by the truck reading the letter with tears streaming down my face. I got my first-time glimpse not only into your heart but also into your mind. Here is what you said.

My Dearest Rachel,

Several things that I have never said that I would like for you to know. I love you more than I have ever loved anyone before, or probably ever will. You have never given me any reason to do any less. If I could settle down and live a normal life it would be with no one but you (if you were willing of course). You are beautiful both inside and out. You have been patient, loving, supporting, understanding, dependable, sacrificing, a good mother and wonderful wife and a lady. I am sorry for our circumstances, and I now realize that they are all my fault. I could never find or hope to find a more wonderful wife than you. I realize what I am as a person. I am a dreamer, a wonderer, I will probably never find happiness in any one place, any one job, I am an adventurous, very spontaneous, and not very reliable. These last few years I have lost my cause, I need a cause to follow to hit hard and finish, then start another cause. I have to wander, experience new circumstances. I have honestly tried to change; I will not, that is me I now realize this. I know that I am responsible and reliable for a while then I get the itch, and I'm long gone, after some non-existent fortune or some useless cause. But I have to try. contentment for me may never exist, but I cannot lie and say that I have it. I am happy but not content, ever changing always seeking something new maybe better maybe worse but at least different. The thing I am most sorry for is the hell I must have put you through by giving you the impression that you are not the sexy-sensual person you are. It wasn't your lack that caused my discontentment but my own nagging guilt of wanting something new and different. Oh, I see women that excite me, but alone at night my thoughts always turn and stay on you.

There are so many concepts and reasons that I would like to share with you but I really don't know how to express them, not to change you because the only change that you need is what you yourself want, I don't want you to be like me you are already a far better person, but that you would get a hint of why I am like I am.

Rachel, I love you, not because your cute, or sexy or sweet, or dependable, or any other reason. Because love is love. It cannot be defined or questioned only accepted. I will always love you and hold you in my heart where no other will ever tread. When I said that the divorce was not a big deal you did not catch my drift. It will not lessen my love for you; nor will it lessen my families love for you. It will however release you from the burden of a dreamer. May God and happiness be your constant companions on your new life and may our friendship never die.

Wayne

Wow! That letter changed everything. You had described how bi-polar affected you better than any book I ever read, we just didn't know it. As I think about that time and the outcome of your letter it put a big bandage on some of my open wounds but there was no real healing. I didn't have the emotional or mental capacity to change my expectations or how I related to you. You shared your soul, and I did not have the ability or understanding of who I was to be able to reciprocate.

I didn't take Nathan on vacation, but he did take me to meet his teacher. I'll never forget how proud he was. He didn't say these exact words, but this was the intent. "See, I do have a mom. Here she is." He was so much his father's son that I didn't know if he would even miss me. One of the ladies from church told me that one evening when he was sitting beside her he said, "You smell like my mom." That made me cry.

Over those few days we had together we renewed our love for each other. It was like falling in love again. We stuck to each other like glue. Though we didn't actually say our vows out loud we committed to never use the word divorce again. I went back to Indiana, gave notice at my job, and packed up my stuff. You came by train and drove us back to West Virginia in our big 1975 orange GMC pickup truck. It still had a West Virginia tag that had expired so we stopped at a rest area on the border of West Virginia and Ohio and waited till dark to drive the rest of the way. We never moved away from West Virginia again.

We knew we wouldn't be able to work on our marriage while living in the basement of your parents" house, so I got a job at the Children's Home in Charleston, and we spent my days off together. When I saw a job opening at the Children's Home in Beckley listed, I applied for it and before it was over we had both been hired and we started the co-ed Semi-Independent Living cottage.

So What?

Heavenly Father,

My journal entry for this decade read, "You were faithful and good when I married Wayne, and we moved and moved and did the best we knew how to do ministry and parent Nathan to love you."

Reliving that decade was important for me to understand that I hadn't been a failure or a disappointment to You. I had been halfway through that decade before my brain was fully developed so that I could begin to make sense of what was happening and You knew that. You knew my narrative was embedded with lies that I didn't even know were there. My heart still wanted to please You, and I still believed that I did that by obeying all the rules. Satan had still been trying hard to use my *Good Christian* box to bury me. However, at the same time, You used that box to protect me and help me remain faithful to you and to Wayne.

Your sovereignty, faithfulness, mercy, omniscience, love, and grace were on full display. I was being conformed to the image of Your Son, and I didn't realize it. There were going to be a lots of twists and turns in the next decade.

Oh, Father thank You for never leaving me or forsaking me.

Amen

CHAPTER THIRTEEN – WAYNE AND RACHEL 2.0

Therefore, there is now no condemnation...
Romans 8:1

The New Normal

With our renewed commitment to our marriage, we settled into our new jobs. Wayne had a new cause to hit hard so he was doing well. The Beckley Child Care Center (BCCC) had never had a Semi-Independent Living program before. Helena was the Social Worker who had hired us, and she quickly became our friend too. Her husband's name was also Wayne and she and I had a lot in common. The three of us quickly set to work drafting and implementing the new program. It was going to be a co-ed cottage with five girls and five guys who were almost eighteen and were getting ready to transition out of the Center to live independently. The organization and creation of the paperwork and records was my strong suit. Interacting and connecting with the kids was Wayne's. We made a great team and the program was successful.

We spent the next three years working together. During the first couple of years, we used the cabin we had down in the country for our days off. During bad weather times we would hang out at Jim and Carol (Wayne's cousin and his wife.) I was not actively involved at church during this time. I was still struggling with trying to please two masters and I choose Wayne. Being on duty 24/7 kept us occupied and I didn't have much time to struggle with my choice. Wayne reached his limit at the three-year mark. It was time to find a new cause.

I'm going to let Wayne tell you about this time.

I took a job enrolling students in long distance truck driving school. Calls came into the main office when someone wanted an appointment. This was before cell phones so after I finished an appointment, I had to find a pay phone and call the office to get my next assignment. Finding houses in the hills and hollows of West Virginia was definitely part of the adventure. I was very successful, and my enrollment rate was very high. I soon got promoted to the main office. I was gone long hours and missed a lot of Nathan's life. I wasn't there for his little league games and other events.

The lady I was working with in the office was very attractive and we were working well together. The day I realized that being in close quarters alone with her was creating a potential situation in which I did not want to get involved - I quit and came home. I really loved and valued you and walked away from the temptation.

I do remember the day in February of that year when your dad died. He had gotten so feeble that men from his church had to help your brother carry him to the car to take him to the hospital. Tim told us that as they were carrying him out, he told the men, "God is still on the throne, and he does all things well." He didn't die from the Parkinson's disease, but it ravaged his body so that when he got pneumonia, he was too weak to fight it.

I was still doing home appointments at that time and the weather was turning into blizzard conditions. The next time I called the office I was told you had called and that I needed to call you. I was sure you were calling to tell me he had died so I just headed home. The roads were getting so bad I followed the salt truck as far as I could coming down the mountain.

We borrowed my grandmother's car and headed out the next morning for the funeral. The weather was still bad, and a blizzard closed the interstate in southern Indiana. We had to get a hotel that night and missed the visitation. We barely made it for the funeral.

Then that August my grandmother died. Nathan was at camp when she died in her sleep. We went to get him and I remember him saying, "That's hard, two in one year." He was eleven at the time.

I'll pick up the story again as I continued working at BCCC until February of 1987. Nathan was in seventh grade when I announced that I had turned in my resignation. We had a mobile home by then and he stood in the hall singing, "Mom's quitting the Center, Mom's quitting the Center." Those years had not been easy for him. We were so consumed with the job that even though he was living right there with us we missed what was happening in his life at school. His fifth-grade year was really bad and changed his school experience forever.

One funny story about him during that time happened in the TV room where the Atari 5200 was. Nate was in there by himself playing one day and I was in the kitchen. All of a sudden, he smacked the machine and said a bad word. I stuck my head around the corner, and he looked up at me so innocently and said, "Those kids are a bad influence on me."

Another Day Another Job

After Wayne's grandmother died, his dad took our mobile home and we moved into his grandmother's house. I got a job as a receptionist/administrative assistant for a home building company. They used day laborers for some of their construction work and my friend was the construction manager. Wayne started working for him and once again he was thriving. He loved to work with his hands and be outside. When he wasn't working for them one of his cousins had some projects that he did for her. It was also during this time that he was really struggling with depression and health problems.

One day I stopped by the Center to visit with a friend. I told her, "I saw your job postings, and I don't want any of them." She laughed and said, "What about this one?" as she showed me a job description for a new position that had just been developed. It was for an Outreach Coordinator, and I was interested. One of the qualifications was I had to have a degree. It didn't matter in what, I just had to have one. They hired me with the understanding that I would get my degree as soon as possible. About the same time there was an opening for a Social Worker in the Boy's Cottage. Wayne got a temporary Social Work License and started working there too.

I love this God story. A couple of years earlier I had considered going back to the school where I had received my diploma because they had become an accredited college. The school was close to where we lived. I went in and talked to my friend who was the registrar. He helped me make a schedule that I could complete in one year. However, it didn't work for me to go then. Now a few years later my friend was no longer there but the plan was in my file, and the current registrar had to honor it. She let me know that her plan would have taken longer.

I got enrolled and was now going to school full time, working full time, had a husband with undiagnosed mental health issues, and a teenage son.

Graduation Surprise

Wayne and Nathan attended my graduation in May of 1988. When we got home, they had a wonderful surprise waiting for me at my desk. A new desk chair and a piece of folded legal pad paper stapled together to make an envelope. Inside I found a card they had made for me. On the front it said, "Can You Believe Rachel Did It?" On the inside it said, "We never doubted her for a second." Signed, Love Nathan and I Love You – Wayne. When I found that card in my treasure box I felt the emotions of that day come flooding back. I'm so glad I kept all those things. It has been so healing to see them and touch them and remember. There had been good fun times in our past.

Training for the Future

While we were both working at BCCC the Boys 'Cottage got a new counselor. As he and I became more acquainted he learned that part of my role as Outreach Coordinator was to help parents learn parenting skills so they could keep their children in their homes. He introduced me to a video based program that was going to be perfect for the parents with whom I worked. I even attended a training seminar to learn how to use the program more effectively. I remember sitting in that seminar and thinking, *I would love to be the one up there on stage teaching others how to use this material.* At that point it was just a dream, but a seed had been planted that would sprout later.

A Change in Wayne

The biggest blessing that came from Wayne's time in the Boys' Cottage was meeting and becoming friends with Billy. He also resumed his friendship with a college friend, Phil. The three of them decided that they were going to get together and discuss the Bible. Wayne wanted to prove once and for all if what he had been taught was true. Phil, who was also having some spiritual struggles, also wanted to prove if it was true. Billy was just confused and wasn't sure what he was trying to prove.

One weekend I had to attend a meeting out of town. When I came home all the magazines and videos were gone from the house. Wayne told me that you had reclaimed our home by telling Satan that he wanted him out of our house and that he was to leave his wife and son alone. He was as happy as I had seen him in a long time.

Billy knew of a church that thought outside of the traditional *Good Christian* box, and we all started attending that church. Billy was at the house often to work out with Wayne. He also loved music, played the guitar and the keyboard. The building beside our house that had been converted into Wayne's workout room was now also a music room.

Over the next couple of years with Billy's help both Wayne and Nathan learn to play the guitar. Wayne started writing songs and learned to use the keyboard presets to add the beat. He spent hours in that room and the songs that poured out reflected all of the spiritual struggle he had been going through over the years. Much of what I know and understand about his heart for God came from those songs he wrote. Eventually we put together a little group called Braided Cord. The name came from Ecclesiastes 4:12, "a cord of three strands is not easily broken." It was just Wayne, Billy, and me when we started. Nathan and his friend became our backup guitar players, and our friend Phil joined the vocals.

During this time my wounded heart kept me from something special. If you remember my music teacher had told my mom that my sister's piano ability came naturally, but I had to work for everything I got. What I got was the ability to do an adequate job playing hymns. What I didn't get was being able to play by ear or grasp how to play cords. I could only play if I had the music. As Wayne continued to write he wanted me to help him. He didn't understand that I didn't know how to help him do what he wanted. He was actually a much better musician than I was. That's where Billy came in and helped Wayne and that's where he felt abandoned by me. I couldn't keep up when he was manic. He could go for hours and hours out there in the music room.

As Wayne's walk with the Lord was rekindled and deepened he was asked to become the pastor of a small church close to our home. The pastor of the church he was attending encouraged him to consider it. Having no idea about his bi-polar, everyone encouraged him to take the position. We followed our usual route of letting circumstances be our guide we made the decision that he would accept the position.

A Treasured Possession

I haven't recounted all the times over the past years that I re-enrolled in weight watchers or tried some other form of dieting. My weight fluctuated frequently but Wayne never said anything negative about it. He didn't have to. My shame attendant said it every time I saw a magazine.

One day not long after graduation when I was at the doctor's office, I saw that they were promoting a liquid fast weight loss product. I signed up and started the program on Thanksgiving Day. I knew if I waited, I'd have more pounds to lose. For the next three months I did not eat any solid food. I drank four shakes a day and ate Jello. I didn't cheat one time (because I had to be perfect) and lost about sixty pounds. I was so proud of myself. I had to buy new clothes, and I looked good. I opened credit card accounts at a couple of stores so I could buy new clothes. Those credit cards were going to come back to haunt us later.

During the time I was doing the liquid fast I walked into my office at work and found an old-style black metal lunch bucket like men would carry into the coal mines sitting on my desk. It was all shiny and had a label taped to the front that said. "I am Rachel Ann Stewart. If I get lost, please take me home to my husband. He can't live without me." Inside was one of my shake packets and a 3x5 card that said "I packed your lunch. You be a good girl and stay out of trouble. I love you, Wayne."

Wayne had found that lunch pail that had belonged to his grandfather in our basement. He spray painted it and put it on my desk at work. I remember how loved I felt that day when I found it. It became one of my most treasured possessions and was one of the items in my memorabilia container from the attic. This was another example of how much he loved me.

I was feeling very proud of my weight loss accomplishments, and I did my fair share of showing off. Wayne had supported me the whole way and was very proud of me too. Then one day I was standing in the kitchen in my little black jeans, and he was admiring me. I now know that the next words that came out of his mouth were not meant to harm me in anyway. He was just commenting on the next step in my transformation. However, they were not received the way he meant them. My locked up damaged heart could not hear encouragement in the words. He said, "Now, if you can just get rid of that little belly." I heard, "NOT GOOD ENOUGH NOW AND YOU NEVER WILL BE!!" I was devastated and I thought, *Why even try? It will never be enough. I'll never match the girls in the magazines.* So I quit trying. I'm not sure how long it took but I gained the weight back.

Truth is I probably would have anyway even without the wound because those lose weight quick diets don't last. The weight loss is not sustainable without a complete change in eating habits. I had not made those changes. I always blamed his statement for why I regained the weight. But that was never true. Another lie uncovered and refuted. He never, ever stopped loving me regardless of how I looked. He knew me better than I knew myself and wanted to encourage me.

Mom Moved In

In March of 1989 my mom came to live with us. She loved Wayne so much and he was her biggest fan. I remember the Father's Day when she gave him a card. As she gave it to him, she said, "I know you aren't my father, but you are a father." She had never given me a Mother's Day card. The first Christmas after we were married, I had given her a double frame with our graduation pictures in it. Her thank you note said, "How did you know that nothing would please me more than a picture of my new son-in-law and his wife." And that never changed. From then on, I had always been "and his wife."

It always upset Wayne anytime we were around my siblings and we started being disrespectful when we talked about Mom. Lorna (my sister-in-law) remembered a time when we had been sitting around the table telling less than affirming stories about Mom. Wayne spoke up and said, "Could we talk about somebody I don't care about so much."
Dear Mom,

I know how much Dad loved you. I have some proof on the 3x5 card I found in your things. Dad had written "I Love You" on it in his shaky Parkinson writing and put it in your suitcase when you were going to the hospital. But I also have memories of times you were the butt of jokes he told in front of guests in our home that I'm sure wounded you although you never let on. One of the ones I remember is when he would tell people, "My wife has lost 25 pounds." Then there would be a dramatic pause, and he would add "five pounds five times." And of course everyone would laugh. I know what that feels like and it's not good.

Dad had only been gone two years when you came to live with us. I had no idea how much you were still grieving your loss. Compassion and empathy were two things that were in short supply from me.

Mom, we were glad you came to live with us. One of the things that writing this book exposed was that you and I never bonded when I was little. Added to that was how my heart locked up when Mr. Davies violated me and I didn't have a warm fuzzy relationship with you. By the time you became part of my daily life I had lots of other wounds too. I knew how much you wanted affection from me. I knew you had to be lonely being home all day by yourself, but I just didn't have the ability to meet those needs. It was taking all I had to give to keep all the balls I was juggling in the air. It was hard to admit but many times I was embarrassed by you.

You made friends easily and all the neighbors loved you. Margaret and Robin loved to have you come over, or they would come and see you. I took good physical care of you and saw that your needs were met but I just wasn't able to engage emotionally. You had Dad's lift chair. I can still hear the sound of the motor letting me know you were coming out of your room to meet me when I walked in the door after work. My stomach would clench. Without the healing I have now experienced, I wasn't able to be assertive and ask you to give me a few minutes when I first walked in the door. Then I would have been able come to your room and visit with you. I had many regrets after you died about things I wished I had done differently. I was able to remind myself that you were in heaven with Jesus and any hurts or slights I had inflicted

167

were healed and forgotten. You loved Jesus so much and were never afraid to tell other about Him.

I loved you the best way I knew how.
Rachel

Resisted Displays of Affection

Dear Nathan,

I know that having your grandma living in our house and sharing your bathroom wasn't easy for you. I didn't have any idea how hard and what wounds you experienced because of it. I do remember some fun things you did for me over the years that I didn't always receive in the way they were intended. Do you remember the time when we lived in Kentucky and I came home from work one day and you were so excited because you had fixed my dinner? You had put peanut butter on some hamburger buns about three o'clock and I got home about 5:15. They were a bit stale, and I did not respond with gratitude and eat your lovely dinner. Then there was the time I came home and when I opened the door you stood there and threw out your arms pointing at the door and said "Tada!" You had brought a little poster home from school and had tried to tape it to the door. You ran out of tape, so you found a hammer and a big nail and nailed it to the hollow door. The nail was sticking out the back of the front door of our rented house. I didn't verbally respond but I'm sure my body language spoke volumes. I still can't believe that you were a latch key kid in kindergarten. What were your parents thinking?

Fast forward to a picture that reminded me of the time you had decorated the house with balloons and banners that said Happy 40th for when I got home from a ladies' retreat. It was really special and funny because it was only my 38th birthday and you knew it. One Sunday I came out of church, and my car had been decorated for my birthday.

Unfortunately, that was one of the times that old wound of being in front of people who were laughing got bumped and I wasn't able to laugh with everyone. You tried and I know there were other times too when I didn't appreciate your efforts. I didn't know then that anytime I was in the spotlight it caused me great anxiety.

I'm so glad that you had such a special relationship with your dad. He got to be the fun parent. Especially those times when he was manic and couldn't sleep and you got to make midnight runs to the Pancake House. My locked-up emotions and my Good Christian box stole a lot of your joy. I didn't know how to teach you discernment either. It had to have been hard to get mixed messages from me and your dad. God knew what parents you needed, and he gave you us. Your teen years had struggles because of Dad's mental health, my physical health, our financial situation, and your own struggles. They made you who you are today; a great husband who adores his wife and she knows it; a dad who loves his kids; a friend who will do anything for those he cares about just like your dad did. It took a while, but you finished your education and are a great educator and caring coach. You have made me very proud to call you my son. I love that I have gotten to know you at a deeper level over the past few years. It's not like any Hallmark movie or novel. It's our own brand of relationship. You know I'm there for you. The next section details the hardest years we had. They started the year you turned sixteen.

Love you, Mom

Spiritual Growth Review

For a couple of years when we were spending weekends at our cabin, or if the weather was bad, with his cousin, I decided that I would just quit going to church too. I thought it would just be easier. I was tired of what I called sitting on the fence. When I was pleasing Wayne, I wasn't pleasing God. When I thought I was pleasing God I wasn't pleasing Wayne. I was so tired of trying on both sides. All you get when you sit on the fence is splinters in your backside.

After we purchased our mobile home and we didn't need to go to the cabin every weekend, I started back to church. I also started doing all the things I believed I was supposed to do. I climbed back in my *Good Christian* box. I participated in Sunday School and even taught one of the adult classes. Many times, when someone complimented me about something I would smile and say, "Thank you," while my thoughts would say, *If they could see my old black heart, they wouldn't say that.*

My job as Outreach Coordinator involved a lot of travel to Charleston. I spent many hours alone in the car listening to several well-known pastors from around the country. The good seeds that were planted inside my *Good Christian* box had been watered and they started to grow. I hadn't known that I was headed for some tough times and what I had been learning and absorbing was going to be just what I needed when the hard times hit. The shame attendant still taunted me with, "You still don't have a quiet time; you are such a hypocrite."

One year I had been asked to speak for one of the sessions at the ladies' retreat. The title that year was *Lord Change Me*. Not only did I not speak but I didn't even go. I was not ready to ask God to change me. I knew that might require something from me that I wasn't ready or willing to give. I was always afraid that if I surrendered everything to God, I could lose Wayne. I didn't know God well enough yet to know that I could trust Him in everything.

So What?

Heavenly Father,

You knew all of this was going to happen and You knew how we would react and respond. It was part of our journey, and You never left us. This part of my spiritual journey is a perfect example of what Paul wrote in Romans 7:19 "For I do not do the good that I want to do, but I practice the evil that I do not want to do." I agreed with Paul when in verse 24 he said "What a wretched man I am! Who will rescue me from this body of death?" That's what my shame attendant wants me to believe - that I am a wretched person with no hope of restoration.

How do I re-story those days? There is no rewind, it happened. But Paul didn't leave himself believing there was no hope. He continues in verse 25 "Thanks be to God through Jesus Christ our Lord! So then, I myself serve the law of God with my mind, but with my flesh I serve the law of sin. I want to do what is right and I don't always get it. The next chapter opens with the ultimate HOPE! And again, I find Romans 8:1 telling me, "Therefore, there is now no condemnation for those in Christ Jesus, because the law of the Spirit of life in Christ Jesus has set you free from the law of sin and death." This verse reminds me that sanctification is a lifelong process. When You say "Rachel, I've always known your heart," it's because You see me in Christ. God, You used everything that happened for our good and Your glory and You aren't done with me. You just keep loving me. You know the storm that's coming, and You will be right there with me in the middle of it.

Amen

CHAPTER FOURTEEN– HARD TIMES STARTED

Rains came winds blew but my house was built on you.
Cody Carnes

It Happened So Fast

The next ten years were the hardest of our lives.

By January of 1991 I had taken the training to teach the original and the teen parenting material. Then I took the training so that I could train other leaders. Taking the training made me eligible to get a commission if anyone I introduced it to bought the program. A plan was in place to offer the training to the Department of Human Services workers around the state; those front line workers who had the ability to impact the parents who were in jeopardy of losing their children. That plan was going well until it became clear that it would be a conflict of interest for me to get the commission and also work as the Outreach Coordinator. After some thought we decided that I would quit my job with the childcare center, and we would start our own business. Wayne would market the training, and I would do the training.

About that same time, Wayne cycled into another bad depression; not able to sleep at night and not able to get out of the bed in the day. We needed to get our publicity materials in the mail so he could do the follow up and set up training.

All that fell on me. I remember being so aggravated with him when I knew he was lying in the bed, and I was in my office working hard to get everything done.

Something Weird Is Happening

It was March when we had our first trainings. I did the one that was local, and we had another training scheduled that was two hours away. The day arrived for that training. I got up early, drove the two hours and got things set up. Not long after I started the training that day, I had started having difficulty talking. I wondered if maybe I was allergic to something in the room and bought some allergy meds on lunch break, but it didn't help. As the session had been finishing up, I started having trouble saying some words. The one I remember specifically was the phrase, tongue in cheek. I couldn't say the word cheek.

As I started home, I stopped for gas and bought a box of Milk Duds. I got on the road and put several candies in my mouth and after about two chews I couldn't chew any more. I had to dig them out of my mouth. Trying to clear my tongue and swallow was also very difficult. That was so strange. By the time I had arrived back home everything was back to normal.

I continued to struggle with chewing and swallowing and if I talked for more than a couple of minutes my speech became very slurred and some words I couldn't pronounce. I made an appointment with my doctor who was married to Wayne's cousin. He knew me personally in addition to being my doctor and I will forever be grateful that he was my doctor. He was a good diagnostician and ordered the blood test that was supposed to confirm what he suspected. The test came back negative but because I was still having the same struggles he referred me to a neurologist.

As I sat in the neurologist's office, he asked me to whistle and say the alphabet. I couldn't complete either task. This confirmed what my doctor had suspected even though the blood test didn't show it. I had Myasthenia Gravis, a rare muscle disease described as, a chronic autoimmune disorder involving your nerves and muscles. Symptoms vary from person to person. "While most people with Generalized Myasthenia Gravis experience muscle weakness and muscle fatigue, these symptoms can range from mild to severe and can affect any part of your body. Symptoms may also fluctuate throughout the day, and from one day to the next. These symptoms can make a variety of familiar activities like climbing stairs, chewing, brushing your teeth, or combing your hair very challenging."[53] While all of that was true for me the most challenging part was the speech; especially since I was not going to be able to be a trainer and that was our business.

At the appointment the neurologist had ordered a battery of tests and a return visit. The day we went back to his office I went armed with lots of questions but every time I tried to ask him one, I would start to cry. He said, "That's ok. If you weren't a little bit depressed, you'd be a grinning idiot" He then prescribed a mild antidepressant.

Fortunately, we had purchased the continuation of health coverage (COBRA) when I left BCCC, so we were not being buried with medical bills. Our other bills were another story. Those credit cards I had gotten and used to buy new clothes when I lost weight came back to bite us.

Even though Wayne attended the next training of trainers' session and tried to keep the business going it didn't work. It soon became evident that I was going to have to apply for disability. I had gone to the local Rehabilitation Services

---

[53] https//www.rystiggo. com

office to see if they could suggest some training I might be able to take that I could do with my limitations. They didn't have any suggestions, so I entered the maze called "Get Approved for Social Security Disability." My first application was denied. I appealed. It was denied. I appealed again.

Part of the treatment plan for the MG was plasmapheresis treatments, a procedure that removes the liquid part of the blood (plasma) and replaces it with albumin. These treatments would provide short term reduction in the symptoms but would not be a cure. I was also being treated with fairly large doses of Prednisone. I remember the day we got the brochure with the information about the side effects of Prednisone. Wayne summed it up this way, "You're going to be hairy, fat and mean." And that's what happened over the next few months. As I became depressed, I turned to sour cream and onion potato chips and miniature Reese Cups for comfort. They didn't comfort but they did help my body balloon to my all-time high weight of over 200 lbs. I was miserable and I felt like such a failure.

Depression Hits Hard

By September our financial situation was very bad. The bill collector calls became so frequent we had our phone number changed. This time the depression was mine. I remember the day I walked across the yard from my in-law's house, and it felt like the weight of the world was so heavy on my shoulders that my knees almost buckled. I thought, *I can't take this anymore*. I went in the house and crawled into bed. The only thing that had kept me out of bed was knowing my mother would be checking on me if I didn't get up. When I did get up all I did was play Solitaire on the computer.

I made an appointment and went to see my counselor. He and I talked about knowing that God was in charge and that he was faithful. I said, as I pointed to my head, "I get it up here, but I can't get it in here," as I pointed to my heart. That's when he asked me if I would consider going to the hospital. I told him we couldn't afford it. He asked if money wasn't an issue would I consider it? I had to ask Wayne. When I got home and asked him, my suitcase couldn't get packed quickly enough. When I told my mom where I was going, she wanted to know if it was her fault. Another example showing that she also had an active shame attendant.

I spent two weeks in the Christian Counseling unit at the hospital that was two hours away from home. The shame attendant was very active. Wayne was just getting back into ministry, and his wife was in the mental hospital with depression. The shame attendant whispered, "What are they going to think." I quickly found out that they were going to think that they loved me and cared for me. The first phone call I got when I was there was from one of the ladies from the church checking on me and encouraging me. I cried like a baby on that phone call.

Group therapy, new depression medication, and time away got me back on track. It was right after I got home when I was out in the car one day that the first poem I ever wrote popped into my head. I pulled the car into a parking lot and scribbled it on a piece of paper.

I Had Lost My Song

Weeks passed by as repetitious actions filled my days.
I couldn't read my Bible, and I couldn't seem to pray.

I began to feel that I had reached my limit.
I didn't see a way that God could possibly be in it.

But worst of all – I had lost my song.

I finally got the help I needed.
I didn't let the warning signs go unheeded.

Time spent away from my usual pattern.
Changed my perspective about things that really
matter.

Two weeks went by as I learned new lessons.
Crying, praying, and reading brought some great
confessions.

I began to see that truly God was with me.
I could go back home content as I was meant to be.

But best of all – God gave me back my song.

Surgery Might Help

My health was not improving even with the medication and other treatments. The next step was surgery. I had been referred to another neurologist in Morgantown at the West Virginia University Hospital. Early in December of 1991 we made the three-hour trip north and I had a Thymectomy, the removal of my thymus gland, a gland I didn't even know I had. For a woman my age it offered the potential for good improvement, but it could take time for it to work.

The surgery was intense. It's the same incision they do for open heart. My breastbone was sawed open and my thymus gland removed. I woke up on a respirator feeling like I couldn't breathe. I started banging my leg on the bed to get the nurses attention. They quickly came and taught me how to work with the machine instead of against it. Shortly after when Wayne got to come in, I took his hand and wrote with my finger on his palm, "NO WIMP." He had to agree. Over the years he had called me a wimp in the pain department.

Five days later I was scheduled to be released, and Wayne and Nathan came to take me home. Things were looking good, and we were just waiting for the doctor to come by and get all the paperwork together. The guys had gone to the cafeteria while I waited. The doctor came in with one of his students, stood beside my bed and said, "You have cancer in your thyroid, what do you want to do about it?" Some bedside manner. I told him I wanted my husband. He paged Wayne, but since Wayne was in the cafeteria and not expecting a page he didn't hear it. The doctor patted me on the hand and said, "I have to go but I'll be back later."

Wayne and Nate were shocked to find me in tears when they returned. As soon as I told Wayne what the doctor had said he went and found the surgeon and learned that the cancer had been removed during the surgery. There was nothing else to do. The neurologist had no business telling me anything about it. So, I was discharged, and we started the three-hour journey home.

Wayne got me all settled in the bed with my pile of pillows when we got home. I learned how to roll to my side so I could sit up and go to the bathroom and not bother him. Just a few days later I started running a fever and we found that a stitch had gotten infected. We went to the emergency room but since the surgery had happened in Morgantown, they didn't want to deal with it, so I was taken back to

Morgantown in an ambulance. Just for the record an ambulance is not a comfortable ride. I spent two days on IV antibiotic and then the ride back home in the car.

At my six-week checkup I was released to go back to work. I quickly found a job using my experience as Outreach Coordinator. That didn't last long because I had really not been ready to go back to work. However, what it did was give me another eighteen months of the COBRA insurance which was very helpful.

It had been eighteen months since I had originally applied for disability. We finally got word that I had a hearing with the law judge to get a decision. The day we went I had my records with me and as we waited I opened the packet. There on the very first page was the information I had given at the Psychiatric hospital when they did my intake. I remember the shame that flooded me when right there on the first page was the information about my molestation as a four-year-old. That old wound was still there leaving me covered in shame once again. I still didn't know it wasn't my shame to bear.

We were called into the room with the judge. There was an employment specialist from West Virginia Rehabilitation there also. The judge asked him if based on my work history and my physical limitations he knew of any job that I could do. His response, "I do not." The judge looked at me and said, "Since you did not use a lawyer, I can tell you right now that you are approved." A load lifted from our shoulders right in that room.

The large navy-blue scrapbook I found in my box of treasures was filled with cards and letters of encouragement that came during these next years. Co-workers, church friends, friends from the past and family supported me during this time.

Another Job Change

All of the stress of my illness made it impossible for Wayne to be bi-vocational. The added stress of the pastorate caused his health to deteriorate, and he had a decision to make. Should he quit his job and just pastor or vice versa? We were in such bad shape financially that he made the choice to resign the pastorate.

Only a few months later and Wayne again quit going to church. He was disappointed and disillusioned about spiritual things. He said, "Every time I try to do the right thing the bottom falls out." This time I had lost my health, we had lost our business, and he just couldn't take it anymore.

We finally received the Social Security back pay, got the bills caught up and my health stabilized enough that I was able to try going back to work. In July of 1993 I got a job working for Mountain State Center for Independent Living. It didn't take long, and I became the office manager in the Beckley office. Things were looking up.

Wayne had been doing some more re-modeling work after he left the pastorate. Being outside and getting lots of physical exercise seemed to be just what he needed. Even his sleeping habits, which had been terrible for years, improved. That quiet period lasted about eighteen months.

Trauma Hits Again

My mom, who was now 84, had been living with us about six years when I had to take her to the emergency room one morning. The next three months were very difficult for all of us as she had three abdominal surgeries in ten days that left her with an ileostomy and no will to live. She spent twenty-one days in intensive care and a couple more weeks in the hospital. There were problems with the ileostomy that required constant nursing care. Unable to come back home she was admitted to an extended care facility.

180

Mom was not improving. The only thing that was keeping her alive was the feeding tube they had inserted while she had been in the hospital. It was incredibly difficult to sit beside her bed every day and watch her suffer. With the help of my shame attendant, I started to believe that Mom was suffering because I hadn't been living for the Lord the way I should. One of God's mercies from that time was the day my brother unexpectedly visited. He lived in Virginia and was on a business trip that allowed him to visit. He helped me see that Mom's suffering had been a result of her body breaking down. God can use those hard times to help us turn to him, but he doesn't cause them. I was able to silence the lie.

Mom had been in the hospital and then the nursing home for three months when she died at the end of October 1995. One of the most special things Wayne ever did for me happened on my birthday that year. My birthday had been on Sunday and Ruth, my sister, had come down and gone to church with me and then we had gone to see Mom. As I stood with my back to the bulletin board that was on Mom's wall Ruth said, "There is a something with your name on it hanging on the board." When I opened the envelope there was a birthday card. While I had been at church Wayne had gone to the store and purchased a birthday card and taken it to the nursing home. There at the bottom of the card in a barely legible scribble was the word, *Mom*. Three weeks later she died. Of course, I still had that card in my memorabilia box, a tangible reminder of how much Wayne loved me.

So What?

Heavenly Father,

My big run on sentence journal entry for this decade read, "You were faithful and good when Dad had Parkinsons and then died and we kept moving and we separated and went bankrupt, got back together and for a time I again chose

Wayne over you and I went back to school and Mom came and lived with us and I developed MG and I struggled with depression and we had no money and Wayne struggled with bi-polar but we didn't know."

Why does any of this matter, everyone has hard times. It matters because while You didn't cause the hard times known as suffering in scripture, You used them in powerful ways. They were the tools You used to continue to conform me to the image of Your son.

I Peter 1:3-9 "Praise be to the God and Father of our Lord Jesus Christ! In his great mercy he has given us new birth into a living hope through the resurrection of Jesus Christ from the dead, and into an inheritance that can never perish, spoil or fade – kept in heaven for you… *though now for a little while you may have had to suffer grief in all kinds of trials.* (italics mine) These have come so that your faith of greater worth than gold, which perishes even though refined by fire – may be proved genuine and may result in praise, glory, and honor when Jesus Christ is revealed."

The shame attendant had worked very hard to bury me in the trials, but You were greater. You knew that my biggest trial and heartbreak was on the horizon, and You were preparing me.

Thank you,

Amen

CHAPTER FIFTEEN – PREPARATION FOR HEARTBREAK

If any of you lacks wisdom, let him ask God, who gives generously...
James 1:5

God's Providence

I didn't know how to start this chapter. I spent the entire day at my desk and did not write one word. I did re-read what I had written many years ago about this time in my life. It was just a record of the facts without any emotion attached but it helped refresh my memory with details I had forgotten. As I sat there, I read the prayer I had taped to my computer monitor. I tried to pray every time I sat down to write asking the Holy Spirit to work fruitfully in my writing. As I ended my day, I reminded myself of the request in that prayer that asked for patience to accept whatever level of fruitfulness or difficulty I had each day. In my mind it had been a day of difficulty. I prayed as I closed things down for the day, "God, you are going to have to help me. I don't know what I'm supposed to write."

Three things happened that evening that showed me how to proceed. I saw a Reel on Facebook (I'll share about that later); I watched the video we were going to discuss in my next Bible study (more about that later too) and I watched a Hallmark movie. I learned something from each one of them that got me unstuck. I wondered, "How does God do that?" I knew and understood as well as I humanly could about God's sovereignty – His absolute right and power to do whatever He wills, without constraint. How God chooses to wisely and purposefully exercise that power is His providence. The events of the evening were not coincidence. They were a providential direct answer to my prayer and another reminder that I have a ***personal*** relationship with the God of the universe. He is definitely incomprehensible. I'm going to start with the movie.

The Movie

How did a Hallmark boy meets girl, boy and girl fall in love movie help me know what to write? Without ever having met Boy, Girl had created a print ad for the men's cologne that would bear Boy's name. Girl had made assumptions about Boy based on what she learned from social media. Boy rejected the ad and would not sign with her company until Girl spent time with him and got to know him. If you have ever watched a Hallmark movie you know how it ends.

As I watched the movie, I realized that my *Good Christian* box had been created based on what I had learned about God from my social media which had included my parents, my Bible college, and the churches I had attended. God was going to continue to dismantle that box. Without even realizing it, He had already been showing me what was true and what had been assumptions. His promise in Jeremiah 29:13 "You will seek me and find me, when you seek me with all your heart," was coming true.

As I was looking though my notes, I came across a page from a notepad where I had drawn a cube and a circle. Beside the cube I had written, restriction and rejection. And beside the circle I had written, provision and protection. The cube was my *Good Christian* box. The deconstruction of that box started in January of 1994, just three months after my mother died.

As I moved through the grieving process of losing my mother, my relationship with the Lord had grown. Even though everything appeared to be good on the outside I struggled as I tried to please Wayne and God. God knew my struggle and He knew what I needed to help with that struggle. He was definitely in it when my pastor said, "Rachel, I'd like for you to start a discipleship Sunday school class for women." What could I say? He didn't know that I believed I wasn't good enough, that God was disappointed in me and that I didn't have the required "Quiet Time." He had watched me as I weathered the storm of my illness, my mother's death, and Wayne's health issues. He didn't know my internal struggle. I wasn't at a place I could share them, so I just said yes.

I adopted a "read through the Bible in a year" program and also read five Psalms and one Proverb every day. That meant I read through Psalms and Proverbs every month. It didn't take long until that daily time with the Lord became something I looked forward to. The Bible I used during that time became a journal as I highlighted and dated verse after verse. I especially marked any verse about trust and then recorded that reference in the back of my journal.

The class was supposed to last for eight weeks and then a new group would start. However, when the eight weeks was up the ladies didn't want to stop. A couple more ladies joined, and we moved into a new study, *Lord I Want to Know You*[54] That was the study that opened my eyes and my heart to what it meant to **know** God. Because I could only read an English translation of scripture, I had missed so much. In biblical times, a name represented a person's character. God's names represent His attributes, His nature. The Sunday before I

---

[54] Kay Arthur, Lord I Want to Know You: A Devotional Study on the Names of God, (Portland, OR: Multnomah Books, 1992)

wrote this chapter my pastor spoke about why knowing the names of God was important.

He said, "I want you to know the God of the Bible deeply, in a way that leads you to worship Him with your whole life. When you are doubting God's power, I want you to know the God who revealed himself to Abraham in Genesis 17 as El Shaddi which means God Almighty. When you are confused about why things are the way they are I want you to know El Elyon, the God Most High of Genesis 14. When you are desperate, I want you to know the God of Abraham in Genesis 22, Jehovah Jireh, which means The Lord Will Provide. When you are sick, I want you to know the God of Exodus 15, Jehovah Rapha which means the Lord heals. When you are fighting battles, I want you to know the God of Exodus 17, Jehovah Nissi, which means the Lord is my victory. When you're weary or wandering, I want you to know the God of Psalm 23, Jehovah Rah, which means the Lord is my shepherd. When you are in your sin and feeling unworthy and coming in repentance, I want you to know the God of Jeremiah, Jehovah Tsidkenu, which means the Lord is our righteousness…"[55]

His words confirmed what I had learned years ago in my study when I had been introduced to all of those names. That knowledge had prepared me for what was coming.

Believing that not having a "quiet time" kept me from having a relationship with God was like believing that because I couldn't do calculus all my other math skills were worthless. Through all my struggles and pain, He had always been, El Roi, The God Who Sees. Not only had I written a poem after my time in the hospital for depression, but I had started writing other things. *Finding Peace in Limbo* was the title of one of those. Rereading that article and a couple others

---

[55] https://mercycharlotte.com/sermons/god-is-good-god-is-great/

exposed the lie that I hadn't had a deep relationship with God. But no matter how deep that relationship had been it could go deeper.

The God Who Provides

The director of the West Virginia American Heart Association came into my office in the fall of 1995 not long before Mom died. She asked me to be the Chairperson for their upcoming Heart Walk. My agency would get exposure at the same time funds would be raised for the Heart Association. After getting the approval of my boss, I agreed. During our conversation she asked me if I knew anyone who would be qualified to be the Area Director. When I learned what the job description was, I told her that I did know someone, my husband. He applied and was hired.

He had just finished up the freelance construction work job he had, and we didn't know what he was going to do next. We saw this as God's providential provision.

Getting off the Fence

My muscle disease, Myasthenia Gravis, had been under control for three and a half years when the stress level at the Center for Independent Living, became too much and I had a relapse. I had been working long enough that I had to reapply for disability. This time it didn't take very long. I was on medical leave while waiting for the decision, so we didn't experience any financial impact.

I had started to journal my conversations with God at the same time I had started reading my Bible every day. I found an entry from March of 1997; *I just don't know about the weight loss issue – is the dissatisfaction with myself from you? From pride? – does the weight really matter???* When I looked at my timeline, I discovered that including the first time I joined Weight Watchers in 1972 I had rejoined six different times. That did not include the two liquid fasts I had tried. I had successfully lost most of the weight I had gained during my time of depression when I had been taking huge amounts of Prednisone and lived on junk food, but I was still not happy with how I looked. I still believed the lie that if I looked like the girls in the magazines, he wouldn't need them.

An entry for April 5, 1997, *As I was lying in bed this morning, I understood the verse that says the joy of the Lord is my strength as never before. Knowing you better and better is something that gives joy no matter what is happening around me. ...This has been some week – Wayne's health – He was sick yet so discouraged he wouldn't go to the Dr ...then when he told me if he didn't feel better on Thursday he would kill himself – I didn't get in a panic – I talked to You. He felt better and we were able to even talk about things we haven't discussed; his fears that I will be sick again and he won't be able to handle it.* (While not able to work I was functional and able to help him.) *How hard the last six years have been for both of us. I haven't acknowledged what it was doing to him. I was taking his strength when I should have been relying on Yours.*

On April 21, 1997, Wayne went to the doctor. He had chronic sinus problems that left him with headaches and elevated blood pressure. He left the doctor's office with antibiotic and a seven-day supply of Ultram for his headache. He could take 1-2 tablets 2-3 times a day. He immediately began to take the maximum dosage. He had been given a prescription to get filled when the samples ran out. It was for 90 pills. Taking 2 tablets 3 times a day this prescription was good for 15 days. The record shows that he told Wayne about the side effects of this medication.

April 22, 1997, *...I didn't compromise with Wayne. I came to the place where I had to choose, and I chose You!* I had gotten off the fence. I made God Lord of my life. That's different than putting him in first place. At the time I didn't remember the illustration I had heard while in college. The speaker said using that terminology would be like him telling his wife that she was first in his life but the little blonde down the street was second, etc. God didn't want to be in first place he wanted to be Lord of my life. He had the ultimate authority over my choices, and I had been making some choices that weren't pleasing to Him. Not making those choices anymore affected my relationship with Wayne.

On May 6th he was back at the doctor's office for his allergy shot and was given another prescription for Ultram, this time for 180 tablets. Enough for 30 days taking the prescribed dosage of one to two tablets every 4-6 hours.

That same day I started leading a weight loss program at church called First Place. It was described as a Christ centered health program with an emphasis on weight loss. The program had nine commitments. My shame attendant jumped on this with both feet. I still had the "I have to be perfect" lie in my narrative so I believed I needed to do this program perfectly or I was wrong and that meant I was bad and would disappoint God. The nine commitments weren't bad. Attendance, encouragement, prayer, Bible reading, scripture memory, Bible study, Live-it plan (aka diet), commitment record, exercise. There was a lot of good information in this program. I was losing weight and so were the other participants. However, as a rule follower I didn't know how to see the program as boundaries with freedom, rather I saw restrictions with shame. That was true of all the times I had joined and rejoined Weight Watchers. I developed an unhealthy relationship with food, always tracking and thinking about what I was going to get to eat next. What would start out well would not be sustainable for me in the long run. The shame attendant was always quick to let me know I had failed again.

The Calm Before the Storm

My MG symptoms were under control, so I was able to help Wayne with his work. I found this entry in his medical records from May 27, 1997. *"Mr. Stewart comes in today with his return appointment. He tells me that lately he has not been doing well at all. He is depressed. He is not eating. He cannot sleep. He feels weak and tired all the time. He has no energy to push himself. He has lost 11 pounds since April 21ˢᵗ. He gets up in the morning, and he feels weak and tired and has no energy to do anything."* This was the first time he was prescribed an antidepressant.

When he returned to the doctor two weeks later, he was still feeling weak, tired, had no energy to do anything. His appetite was poor. But he did report that he thought the antidepressant had helped him some. By the middle of June, Wayne told the doctor that he was feeling much better. His appetite was better. Generally, he was feeling better. He was sleeping and resting better. I was still helping him with his work, and we were able to enjoy some time together.

Every summer there was a reunion for all the people who had ever called Prosperity, West Virginia their home. Many of Wayne's family came for that weekend. Every year one person was honored for their contributions to the community. This was the year his dad was being recognized. Wayne was feeling pretty good but had lost a lot of weight and with it a lot of his strength. The previous summer he had been bench pressing over 400 pounds and this summer he was having trouble lifting a folding table. He was very discouraged, and his health continued to decline. He saw the doctor every week for his allergy shot. However, his blood pressure was always very high, and he felt so bad that they would give him a shot of antibiotic and an anti-inflammatory instead.

Two of his friends from college days had contacted him and were coming to see him. We didn't know why they were coming but Wayne said maybe they could show him something about God he hadn't ever seen before. At the same time, Rick, one of his friends from high school had contacted him. They had lost contact because Rick had been in a high-level security position and hadn't been able to be in touch with anyone.

Winds are Picking Up

Friday, July 18th we took Wayne to the emergency room. He was having muscle spasms and could not sit still. He started having trouble breathing. He ran out of the house to the little building beside the house where he lifted weights and wrote his music. The door was locked. While I ran back to get the key he kicked in the door.

He was freezing, wearing a hooded sweatshirt and a winter coat, and still shaking when we got to the ER. They asked if he did drugs because it looked like withdrawals. We said no but we were very wrong.

I discovered some heart breaking information as I was excavating this period in my life. In April the doctor had given Wayne the sample of Ultram (the brand name for Tramadol) for his headaches. He was told that it was a non-narcotic pain reliever for mild to moderate pain. It was in fact an opioid that had been approved by the FDA just two years before in 1995. It didn't become a controlled substance until nineteen years later in 2014. The samples helped so the doctor gave him a prescription for "1-2 tablets 2-3 times a day." That was how often he was taking the medication. What we discovered when we tried to get it refilled was that the insurance would only cover it at a much lower dosage. He had been without the medication for a couple of days when we took him to the ER. He was experiencing withdrawal, and he had become dependent on the medication. He spent the whole night in the ER and early in the morning after giving him something to calm him down they sent him home and we never knew what had happened to him until now. Later that morning, Saturday, July 19th his friends Tim and Paul came for their visit. They spent the whole day together and Tim and Paul never knew anything had been wrong.

Monday, July 21[st,] our 25th wedding anniversary, we went to the doctor. The doctor couldn't find anything physically wrong with Wayne and asked if he would be willing to see a psychiatrist. After jumping through the insurance hoops, we were able to get an appointment with a psychologist. She told us this situation was out of her league, and she referred us to a psychiatrist at the university medical center an hour away that she said was very good. We were never able to see her but were finally given an appointment for the 25th of August with a different doctor. Wayne and I spent many hours going over his history as we filled out the required paperwork. He didn't have the strength to fill it out, so he talked and I did the writing. We had to dig into the past and try to remember things about his childhood and information about his family members. This was very draining for him. I don't remember what the question was, but this was his answer. "I am very tired of feeling bad and while I don't make plans to end my life I wouldn't care if it did. In fact, that would be my preference."

We were trying to hang on. Life had become more difficult for Wayne to work and function. He did just what was absolutely necessary to keep his job. The rest of the time he was either in bed or down in the basement by himself. It was during this time that he had his annual evaluation and for the first time in his life he got one that was less than stellar and that really discouraged him. As with any fund raising job, they want you to do more and more. He was working as hard as he could to accomplish what he had and now they wanted more.

After all those hours filling out the paperwork the doctor told us up front when we got to our appointment that he hadn't read them. He said he didn't want to have any preconceived ideas. We spent an hour and a half with him. The paperwork we had filled out had his full name. Even though we told the doctor he went by Wayne, he called him Carl the whole time. He was a resident from another country, and we had a hard time communicating with him. At the end of our time together he told us that he was almost certain that Wayne was bi-polar or manic depressive. He wrote him some prescriptions and told us to get a book. He knew the last name of the author and a partial title and that was the end of the visit.

The book was not readily available in a store or at the library, so we ordered it. In the meantime, we got on the internet and started reading what we could find. As we read, we were convinced that the doctor had made an accurate diagnosis. Having a diagnosis helped Wayne understand what had been going on all these years but it also discouraged him to think that he was going to have to fight it the rest of his life. One article talked about the "roller-coaster life and the helplessness to control emotions" that manic-depressive patients endure. That was an accurate description of Wayne's life. As we worked together to fill out the questionnaire he realized that he had been fighting this most of his life. All of the information we read indicated that this illness could be controlled with medication. However, it could take some time to get the right medicine and the right dosage. We didn't realize it, but we didn't have much time.

My journal entries indicate I was clinging to the Lord, staying in the Word, and trusting Him. August 27th *Satan wants me to be discouraged. It all seems to be piling in. Wayne makes statements like "I'm through with God." All this new stuff – Bi-polar – still the headaches. But our honesty level is so much better – no hiding things. Some are hard to hear but need to be said and aired. It is what it is, and life is hard for everyone, You promised it would be – but we have heaven to look forward to – John 16:33. We know how the story ends – We are overcomers! You keep reminding me that You love me and I keep trusting You.*

Wednesday, September 17th *Wayne continues to have a difficult time. He is becoming more agitated as time goes on. I have a call in to the Psychiatrist."* Wayne told me that it was becoming more difficult for him to control his impulses. He had always had a tight rein on his anger. He doesn't want to hurt anyone and that is part of the reason he stays in the basement. The doctor called back and gave us an appointment for Friday.

Thursday morning, September 18th *journal entry Psalm 94:18-19 "When I said, "my foot is slipping," your unfailing love, LORD, supported me. When anxiety was great within me, your consolation brought me joy."*

Category 5 Approaching

I had a doctor's appointment out of town that Thursday. After the appointment I spent some time with a friend, so I was gone most of the day. I had gotten stuck in traffic on the way home so my plans to be gone that evening had changed. When I got home Wayne was sitting in his chair and I could tell that he didn't feel well at all. He had been trying out different scenarios all week that included selling the house and moving to a different climate, changing jobs, us splitting up and him moving away. So, I flippantly asked him, "Have you made any life changing decisions today?" He responded, "Maybe, I do know that these have been two of the most miserable days of my life."

He had been without pain medication for two days and was once again heading into withdrawal. The prescription had to be rewritten not just refilled and the doctor who had been prescribing it was out of town. I had called the covering doctor on Tuesday, and she wouldn't submit the refill. When I talked to her on the phone she said, "anyone in that much pain should see a doctor." Wayne responded, "What does she think I have been doing all this time.?" He wouldn't go to the clinic.

When I found this note from the doctor in Wayne's medical record, I finally understood why she wouldn't refill his prescription. "*9/16/97 11:25 AM Received message pt. wanted Ultram called in. Pt has taken 450 tablets in 35 days. Called the pharmacy who states to take only 8 tabs a day which equals 250 in 35 days. Pharmacist also states this causes damage to his body. I called wife and told her I could not call this medicine in and the pt needs to see a doctor if he is in this severe of pain.*"

I had also called the psychiatrist and told him the situation, and he said it was the family doctor's job, and he wouldn't write the prescription either. Wayne was standing in the living room when I told him what the psychiatrist had said. I can still see him as he threw up his hands and said, "That's it. I will never see another doctor as long as I live. They just want my money; they don't care about me."

Something else I found out from my research was that using Tramadol for 10 or more days a month could trigger rebound headaches. Rebound headaches develop when a medication that's supposed to treat headaches lead to more frequent or worse headaches. Wayne had first been prescribed Tramadol on April 14, 1997. So, he had been taking it regularly for five months. The headaches which had become debilitating had been caused by the medication he was taking to treat them. But I didn't know that until now.

Back to that Thursday afternoon.

A little while later when I asked him about selling our bicycles to one of the neighbors he replied, "I don't care what you do with them I won't ever be using them again." Shortly after that he went downstairs. I went to check on him, and he was boxing up some things in the garage. When I asked him what he was doing he said, "Just getting rid of some junk." I went back upstairs and watched TV for a little while then went to check on him again. This time he was at his computer. I said, "Why don't you come upstairs with me, and we can lie on the bed so you can relax. He replied, "I am so tired, and I hurt so much I just need to be alone." I laid my head on his shoulder and caught a glimpse of the computer screen just before he deleted what he had been writing. I saw the sentence that said, "All the love in the world can't stop the pain."

I started to put the pieces together and realized what he might be planning. I started thinking about who I could call that he would talk to. I couldn't think of anyone. I was getting frantic in my mind and asking God what to do. As clearly as if he had said it out loud, I heard, "Leave him alone. He has to make his own peace." I had been trying for years to step in and make bad situations go away. God let me know this was a battle I couldn't fix. I went back upstairs and started praying.

In a few minutes he came upstairs and changed his clothes. He told me he was going out for a little while. I begged him, "Please let me go with you. I'll drive." He said, "No, I just need to be by myself." He walked across the room, kissed me on the cheek, and left. I heard the truck leave the driveway but, in a few minutes, I heard it come back, and I heard him come in through the basement door. I ran to the top of the steps and asked, "What are you doing?" He said, "I forgot to get my duct tape, everyone needs duct tape in their truck." Then he said, "Can I bring you anything?" and left.

I started pacing the floor, praying for him, and asking God what I could do. I didn't know what to do. I couldn't call the police; he hadn't done anything wrong, and I didn't know where he was going or his license plate number. I wanted to call his family but if he came back and I had all of his family worked up he would really be mad. I finally called my brother in Virginia and told him that Wayne had left and that I didn't know where he was and that I was afraid he was going to hurt himself. They did the only thing they could do. They prayed with me, and they spent the night praying.

Nathan was at work at Papa John's. When he got home about 3 AM I told him, "Your dad left and hasn't come back and I'm worried." He said, "Oh, Mom, he does that sometimes." I replied, "No this isn't typical behavior, and I'm worried about him." I had told him earlier in the week that his dad was a time bomb. He was either going to hurt himself or someone else. Nathan tried to get me to go to bed and said that he would wait up for him. Of course, I couldn't do that and eventually Nathan went to his room.

Throughout the rest of the night, I alternated between pacing the floor and reading all the verses I had underlined in Psalms that I had listed in the back of my prayer journal about trust. I often told the ladies in my Sunday school class "If you are fretting you aren't trusting." I tried to practice that. I stood in the guest bedroom watching out the window that overlooked the driveway hoping and praying that his truck would pull in. While I was standing there I ironed "that boy's" shirts one last time.

As daylight crept upon the horizon, I knew that the sound I was listening for was no longer his truck. Instead, I was listening for whomever would be coming to tell me they found Wayne. I found my journal and penned these words: *Wayne has been gone all night. I don't know where he is, but you do and you can protect him. I am putting my trust in you*

*and hiding in you, my refuge. Philip and Lorna are bringing
him before your throne. Thank you for them. Whatever
happens I want you to get the glory.*

The Hurricane Made Landfall

Almost twelve hours passed before a vehicle pulled into
the driveway. As I looked out the door three men all dressed
in shirts and ties exited the white jeep. As one of them passed
in front of the vehicle sunlight reflected from the badge he
was wearing on his belt. All my hopes were immediately
dashed and the sound I heard was from deep inside my soul
where my heart had just broken into a million pieces.

I called to Nathan, "The police are here, the police are
here." We met them at the door as they came up on the porch.
I said, "You've found my husband, haven't you?" They said,
"Yes." "He's dead isn't he," I said. "Yes," they said. "I knew
it, I knew it. I knew he was going to do it." I grabbed Nathan
and he held me as we cried together. In the back of my mind
as I wondered how we would survive I knew that somehow
God would help us. I just didn't know how. What I didn't
realize at that moment was that God had been preparing me
for this moment of trauma all of my life. God's Word says in
Psalm 147:3 That "He heals the broken-hearted and binds up
their wounds." And that is exactly what immediately started
to happen.

A trauma is a wound that is violently produced. Wayne's
suicide violently broke our hearts and traumatized our family.
People who are traumatized are in shock and need of
immediate treatment. One of the first things you do for a
trauma victim is to immobilize them. Bandages can be used
to immobilize, support, and protect. They keep out dirt and
germs and hold the wound together so healing can take place.
They are to be applied snugly to ease the pain but, not too
tightly or they will interfere with circulation. The first

bandages that were applied to my broken heart and helped immobilize it came in the form of family.

Most of Wayne's family lived right beside me so within minutes Nathan and I were being held by Wayne's dad. However, his heart had been broken too. Many times, when there is an accident, the wounded treat each other until the professionals can get there. That is what happened, initial first aid was administered by those who were hurting too. We as a family drew together and held each other until others arrived who could better administer care.

I remember standing in the kitchen with my father-in-law and son while the detectives were still there and feeling that I was watching what was happening from outside my body. I watched myself crumple to the kitchen table with my head on my arms sobbing. I watched as the detectives told Nathan about when we would be able to get Wayne's personal effects and his truck. I watched as I hugged Nathan and asked him how we were going to live without Wayne. I watched as I begged someone to take me to the hospital so that I could see his body. To this day I don't know why that was so important to me, but I needed to do it.

Wayne's dad, Carl, went home to start notifying people. Nathan took me to the hospital. By the time we got home there were people waiting for us. Some of the "professionals" had arrived, friends from church. With each new arrival there was another round of tears. The "Reel" I had watched on Facebook as I was getting ready to write this chapter discussed the physical benefits of tears. They flush out cortisol, our stress hormones, and activate the endorphins that are the body's natural mood booster and pain reliever. Tears and lamenting mitigate depression by expressing it in a healthy way. They help regulate our nervous system, so we don't stay in fight or flight mode, and our bodies get the message that we are safe. And last, they open up our soul to healing. There was a lot of cortisol and endorphins flowing in that kitchen that day.

When we got home my brother from Virginia had arrived. It wasn't long before Nathan's fiancé arrived from college. She had already become part of our family and was deeply feeling the loss also. Her love and attention were the bandages Nathan needed around his heart.

As the day progressed, I continued to remember people that I needed to call. There was something therapeutic about doing this myself. There were friends from college days with whom we had stayed in touch. There were people from all the different places we had lived during our twenty-five years together. Everyone was shocked to hear the news and offered their sympathy and prayers. All of those things continued to bind the bandages around my heart.

My brother from Colorado was making plans and would be there the next day. Family and friends had been notified, and people were stopping by. No one could believe it. Nathan, who was twenty-two, stepped up and started taking care of things. He had lost his father and his best friend.

Later that afternoon he drove up in the yard in his Jeep and asked me to come outside. The license plate on the front bumper proudly proclaimed, "Wayne's Boy." More tears.

My best friend from college lived in North Carolina. She was there the next morning and handled everything at the house; the phone calls, the food, and the visitors. I was surrounded with love and care. With God's help and that of family and friends I was going to be able to walk through the next few days of pain and agony.

The Funeral

There had been many times in my life when funerals seemed very barbaric. However, I had learned that they weren't barbaric. Funerals were part of the healing process.

Wayne died on Friday. The earliest my brother from Colorado could get to West Virginia was Sunday. There were relatives from out of state that were making their way as well. God had also provided a way for several of my dearest friends from college days to be able to be with us. With friends and family surrounding us we moved through the next few days still in shock with each of us trying to understand how this had happened and trying to help his friends and family understand.

When the only person Nathan wanted to lead his dad's funeral was going to be out of town, he decided that he would have to do it himself. He said, "Mom, I have to do it, I'm the only one who really knows. I have to do it." I made sure he knew that it would be very difficult, but he was adamant that he was the one. He let everyone know that anything anyone wanted to write about Wayne would be read at the service. Or, if anyone wanted to speak they could.

Many of Wayne's family and friends had written beautiful things about Wayne. Many people also got up and shared from their heart about what he had meant to them. We moved to the cemetery and my pastor shared briefly from Romans 8:39 "For I am convinced that neither death nor life, neither angels nor demons, neither the present nor the future, nor any power, neither height nor depth, nor anything else in all creation, will be able to separate us from the love of God that is in Christ Jesus our Lord." He offered everyone the assurance that because Wayne had given his heart to the Lord many years before that he was in the presence of God. He reminded us that suicide was covered in the list of things that could not separate us from God.

As I sat in the car waiting for the others to join me so we could go back to the funeral home a statement started playing in my head over and over. I just kept thinking, *I don't want him to be dead. I don't want him to be dead*, over and over.

My heart felt like a lump of cold hard clay in my chest. It would be a few weeks before I realized what the true meaning of those words of despair really meant.

So What?

Heavenly Father,

I found out from experience that Your promise in Psalm 34:18 is true. "The LORD is near to the broken-hearted and saves the crushed in spirit." My heart was truly broken, and I was deeply crushed in my spirit.

It was no accident that as it was time to write this chapter the Bible study lesson video *Getting Through What You're Going Through*[56] was about grief. You knew I was going to walk through this hard time once again and that old wounds would be touched. Hearing Rick Warren talk about what he learned about grief when he lost his son to suicide reminded me of things I had learned all those years ago.

I had known that I was going to have to go through grief and that it was best to try not to avoid it. What I hadn't heard before was what he said about loss. He said that there is no life without change. Change is inevitable and in order for there to be change there has to be loss and that loss brings pain. But the way through the loss and pain is grief and that is a choice.

Understanding that sadness was not a weakness went against what I had learned as a child about not showing emotions and it not being okay to cry. All the entries in my journal where I asked You to not let me cry showed I hadn't learned that truth. I had asked that because I didn't want anyone to think I was weak. And it was true what my mom had said that when I am shown sympathy I tear up. That is still true today and I'm learning to be okay with that because I

---

[56] https://saddleback.com/watch/how-to-get-through-what-youre-going-through

know it's how You made us, and our tears have healing power. When Mary and Martha were crying about the loss of their brother Lazarus, You cried too.

I liked being reminded that because You are close to the broken hearted, I know that You grieved with me then and You grieve with me even now as I find the areas of my heart that hadn't already healed. My emotions come from You, God.

Grief is healed in community. My friends and family who surrounded me and later the *Growing Through Grief* workshop I participated in are evidence of this truth.

And last but definitely not least is that grief takes time; that I couldn't fix it for me or for anyone else; that I wouldn't get over it; I would get through it. And, I am still getting through it, one day at a time.

You never left me for one moment. You continued to bandage my broken heart with scripture. As I re-read my journal, I see that my questions and my anger and my tears have all been part of the healing process. You were and always will be with me, as Jehovah-Rapha: The Lord Who Heals, every step of the way.

Thank you,
Amen

CHAPTER-SIXTEEN – PICKING UP THE PIECES

My soul is weary with sorrow; strengthen me
according to your Word.
Psalm 119:28

The Source of My Security

Steve Brown, in his book, *Approaching God*, tells about the time when during a hurricane while he was hiding in a closet with the roof falling into the house his dog, Quincy, had come into the closet with his ball in his mouth. Quincy dropped the ball into his lap and started wagging his tail wanting to play. Steve said, "Quincy, you stupid dog! The house is falling apart. We are going to die! This is not the time to play catch."

Steve wrote, "Quincy didn't understand that. As long as I was there, as long as the source of all his security was there, as long as he trusted me, the hurricane didn't matter."[57]

Reading Steve's book when it had first been published in 1996 had been part of God's preparation for me so that I could withstand the hurricane that had just swept away my husband. In my heart, underneath all the pain, I believed that the source of my security was in my Heavenly Father, and I would survive.

One week later my journal read, *"Wayne never came home to me. But he is with You, and You will be able to take much better care of him than I ever could."* Isaiah 7:9 was

---

[57] Steve Brown, Approaching God, How to Pray, (Nashville, TN: Moorings, 1996) pg. 56

part of the scripture I read that day, "If you do not stand firm in your faith, you will not stand at all." There was a bandage for my broken heart. The next day I read Isaiah chapter 9:1, "Nevertheless there will be no more gloom for those who were in distress." That verse seemed to say to me, "I've got him, and he is okay." If ever there had been someone in distress it had been Wayne.

View From My Box

I often sang at church. I would hear a song on the radio that really spoke to me, I would learn it, then sing it and share my testimony about what it meant to me and why. *Whatever It Takes,*[58] is the title of one of the songs that I sang with all my heart several times. *"And whatever it takes, to draw closer to You Lord, that's what I'd be willing to do, and whatever it takes for my will to break, that's what I'll be willing to do."* As I excavated this decade, I discovered old wounds that had been covered up but never healed. Thinking through this song exposed one of those wounds. The verses of the song listed many things that I told God I was willing to let Him take if it meant I would be closer to Him. Things like my houses and land, my dreams, and my plans. But the one that came back to haunt me said "Take the dearest things to me, if that's how it must be, to draw me closer to thee…"

I had been praying this long before we knew about the bi-polar. What I had really been asking was for God to get him back in the box with me. I wanted my happily ever after that included us going to church together and doing all the right things. Writing those words makes me sad and angry. Sad for all the years I lost not seeing the wonderful man who was in such deep pain. Angry that I didn't understand that the lies

---

[58] https://www.youtube.com/watch?v=Ghr4GiFYU8M&list=RDGhr4GiFYU8M&start_radio=1

from my shame attendant had kept me from the relationship I could have had with Wayne.

As the days went by, I began to realize that when I was saying at the cemetery that day, "I don't want him to be dead" what I really meant was, "I didn't mean for him to die." When I said, "Take the dearest things to me" I didn't mean for Wayne to die. Why did I even believe that was a possibility? Because I had misinterpreted stories I had heard in the parsonage as I was growing up. Stories about how God had used things that happened in people's lives to "draw them closer." I now understand that using something that happened is vastly different than causing something to happen.

I quickly made an appointment with my counselor to talk about what I had discovered. He assured me that even if that was what I had prayed, God wouldn't answer a prayer like that. I heard what he said, and it was a bandage on a wound but that's all it was then. Just a bandage, and bandages don't heal. Now, exactly 28 years later to the day, I'm able to pull that bandage off. What I can see now is a healed wound that left a scar. I can say with confidence that in those painful, hard moments God saw my heart. Those cries from my heart were taken to the Father for what they truly were; the desire to love God with all my heart and soul.

Romans 8:26-27 confirms what my counselor said. "…the Spirit helps us in our weakness. For we do not know what to pray for as we ought, but the Spirit himself intercedes for us with groanings too deep for words. And he who searches hearts knows what is the mind of the Spirit, because the Spirit intercedes for the saints according to the will of God."

View From a Friend

Wayne had a best friend named Phil. They spent many hours together over the years discussing things he could never talk to me about because I was so firmly in my *Good*

Christian box. I asked Phil to tell me about Wayne from his perspective. Here are some excerpts that gave me a good picture of Wayne and echo many of my wishes too.

Wayne's work ethic, study ethic, family ethic, and play ethic all shared a common enthusiasm. He was all in on pretty much everything he did, and it wasn't long before he excelled at it, especially if it was anything physical or athletic.

Over time, it became clear that there was something driving him, and sometimes beyond his limits. In the weight room endless hours of pressing the massive weights to the breaking point. Projects, or studying that would be all-nighters, became the norm.

I wish, I wish, I wish that I had understood more of the physical torment, the mental torment, and spiritual torment he was going through. I confess that I struggle with understanding why God allows bad things to happen to good people, especially His children.

I get it...that free will means freedom to choose, from unlimited choices, in a cursed world.

But I also believe that God intervenes, responds to prayer, and sometimes puts a hedge of protection about us. But I do struggle to understand the choosing criteria that is used by a God of love, that allows tragedy, suffering, and heartache to those that he loves.

Phil continues, *"I also am baffled at how ministry workers can be so harshly treated, and mostly by other believers, and in many ways making it a very thankless job.*

I know from many hours of discussion that Wayne struggled with many of these same issues. He spent countless hours studying the Bible and praying, seeking answers and guidance. Wayne loved the Lord, was serious about his faith, but was frustrated with meaningless rituals, or judgemental people. He had low tolerance for Christians that had a mold that they expected other Christians to fit perfectly into, conforming their warped view of what a Christian should look like, talk like, act like. [Even though that described me, Wayne understood my heart. He understood how I had learned to live in that box, and he loved me deeply.]

I firmly believe that Wayne's actions in the final days were motivated (no matter how misguided) by a selfless desire to protect the ones he loved.

I could not imagine living with no diagnosis, misdiagnosis, meds that didn't work but had very bad side effects, lack of treatment, sleepless nights, and all the while trying to keep it together for your family. He hid it pretty well from most, but the ones closest lived the good and the bad, and that, he told me, bothered him the worst.

Guilt, I have none, because that would imply that I had ill will, or bad intentions towards my brother, and I had none!

Regrets I have many…should have known more, done more, loved more, been there more, supported more, been available more….

There is still an empty space in my heart, that when visited, is lonely and dark, but I force myself to remember the music, the golf outings, the talks, working together, a heart of gold and I see his smile as he lifts 1000 pounds over his head, and that brightens my mood.

The View from More Friends

The cards and letters in the second scrapbook I had in my treasure box confirmed Phil's assessment of Wayne. Several of the letters were written by his American Heart Association co-workers. Being reminded of what an incredible man Wayne was and having the "not good enough" lie refuted brought more healing.

Kathy wrote, "Every time Wayne came to our office his smile and soft spoken voice was a soothing effect." "It is so amazing that one person could have so many kind and loving family and friends," was written by a co-worker who attended his funeral.

His boss wrote, "Wayne was loved and admired by many friends, volunteers and colleagues and will be greatly missed. His kindness and thoughtfulness touched the hearts of all who knew him." Another Kathy wrote, "He spoke often of you and how very much you meant to him. I told my husband recently that I could only hope to have that kind of open affirmation of one's love for his mate."

Pam said, "Another part of Wayne, I remember is how much he loved you and Nathan. He spoke of both of you often." And finally, Mike let me know, "Rachel, Wayne loved you too, with all his heart…"

Wayne was gentle, kind, and compassionate and he loved others well. As I have been excavating this difficult decade of my life my shame attendant wants me to live in the regrets and feel shame. I can easily echo Phil's words, regrets I have many…should have known more, done more, loved more, been there more, supported more, been available more….

But the truth is those words aren't really true. I knew as much as was available at the time, I did everything I knew to do. I loved him with all of my heart the best way I knew how. I tried to support him in everything he did, and I always tried to be available. However, living in my box made life hard for both of us.

A Poem and Pictures

A reminder of his love I found in my treasure box was the poem he wrote me one year for our anniversary. His words refute the regrets.

God's intent from the beginning
Was for a man to have just one wife
That they would bond to each other

To love and cherish one another all through life

We've been together for some time now
We've fought every battle and we've won
If I could start all over and begin my life anew
I would do things different, but I would still choose
you

I know it's not been easy at times
We've worked hand and hand, and we made it
through
The Lord has kept us faithful to each other
I love you and forever will be true

I still look forward to the future
New things to share together you and I
You have given me a life to remember
I need you and I'll love you till I die

Every year my father-in-law hosted a New Year's Day breakfast. Part of that tradition included family pictures. Every year, no matter how much I weighed, Wayne's arm was around me and the look on his face said love. How did I miss that? I was so consumed with wondering how fat I looked in the pictures that I missed the most important thing – the look he had for me that said, "I love you."

And Then There Was Anger

There was anger when it took three days and three tries to get his truck back from the police. There was anger when the Psychiatrist called as I walked in the house from the funeral. When I had called on Wednesday to tell him Wayne was having a hard time he gave us an appointment for Friday.

Early in the conversation he said, "I waited on him for an hour on Friday." The tone of voice I used when I replied could be described as a hiss when I said, "He couldn't come. He was dead."

And there was anger with the man from the cemetery. Based on my experience two years before when my mother died, I was expecting to hear any day that his marker had been put in. It had been about a month when he finally came to the house on his "follow up visit." I quickly discovered that the marker had not been ordered, and I erupted. We moved past that, and he began to ask me questions about how the cemetery personnel had done their jobs that day. I quickly informed him, none too gently, that I was the wrong person to ask that question. The cemetery was right across the street from the funeral home, and his next question was about how traffic control had been that day. More anger. Why would the person who had just buried their loved one be asked about traffic control on the day of the funeral? I responded with so much anger that I went to his office the next day to apologize. I also let him and the people he worked with know that they should NEVER again ask those questions to the person who had just buried someone.

WHY?

As the shock wore off I started to feel and think again. Three weeks later on October 8th my journal entry said, *"Questions are bubbling - How do I make the pieces fit? I know you were there all the time. If part of his problem was the illness, why didn't we find it? I believe he truly wanted to do right, why couldn't he find the answer? I keep getting assurance of your presence. I thank you for that. Think on the good things you told me this morning. I can't ever go back and change anything, but do I need to understand more? I keep hitting a wall when I try to get info."*

October 29th, I wrote, *"Lord – I'm in pain this morning. I miss him so much. I know you have him, and he is okay, but I want him here with me. I don't understand but I'm trusting you. I know this is all part of the process, but do you know what? I HATE IT!!!"*

November 11th, *"Another day survived. I hope Pastor remembers I need to talk to him. I'm confused. I know I really hurt and am sad but how do I keep the depression away? I want to please you, but I just want to curl up and cry too. Can I do both?"* The answer to that question was absolutely. It was the lies from the *Good Christian* box that made me think it wasn't okay to curl up and cry. I didn't know about the physical benefits of crying.

November 13th, *"Talked to the pastor yesterday. He made a good point that I have to leave the questions about how, why, and what if I want to move on. He said, "Rachel, even if God sat down beside you right now and gave you all the answers it wouldn't change anything. Now, what are you going to do with the rest of your life?"* (That was good advice, but it took time for me to get to the place I could follow it.) The entry continued, *"I don't want to be depressed. I don't want people to worry about me. How do I hurt so badly and still try to do for others? I guess it's just one minute at a time like always, isn't it? Just resting, trusting, missing, hurting, resting, and trusting."*

The next day I wrote, *"Had a hard time getting up today. I've lost my purpose right now… I think I'll just be still and remember that you're still God and you know and understand. I don't and won't until eternity."*

I could walk you through entry after entry as I tried to find my way. But those details aren't necessary. I was still firmly in my *Good Christian* box and even though I was in the Word most days and was praying it was from the perspective of my box. God had plans for me. He knew my heart and what I would need to make that happen. I'm going to talk to him about it.

So What?

Heavenly Father,

You saw the dad who had lost his son and the son who had lost his dad and best friend. You saw the wife who had lost her husband and the soon to be daughter-in-law who lost the man she admired and was looking forward to having as a father-in-law. You saw the siblings who had lost their brother and all the cousins, aunts, neighbors, best friends, co-workers, and boss who were grieving the loss of Wayne. You knew that it was hard not to bump each other's pain unintentionally. You saw the misunderstandings and unmet expectations as we all tried to move forward.

You knew I believed I had to be perfect and that included how I grieved. It didn't take much to bump my pain during those days and there were days when what spilled out wasn't very pleasant. It could be a song on the radio or driving by our favorite restaurant that would bring the tears. It could be times I ran into a friend who didn't know. I was trying to be strong for everyone. *They will think...* was always in the back of my mind. I made decisions based on what I thought others would think. Those were the decisions that got me into some very difficult situations and spilled some ugly responses.

As the months went by You saw me spend time visiting places I used to live and visiting family trying to find a place to call home. I felt restless, sad, hollow, and abandoned. Then on my trip to Colorado I found it. I remember the day I was in the car with my brother Tim as we drove down the mountain from Manitou Springs. There lying in the valley before me was Colorado Springs and I immediately fell in love. I said, "I could live here." And I did. In just three months I was packing the U-Haul and heading west even though I didn't know anyone in Colorado Springs. I knew that I could find a church, and I would find friends. You knew that I would never be able to dismantle my *Good Christian* box if I stayed where I was. It was going to take a long time, but it started with this move.

You know that it was during my many sleepless nights that I started writing. I also did two things I never thought I would do before I left for Colorado. I went rappelling and I went whitewater rafting. I wrote about both of them. The piece about rappelling was in my first book. The piece about whitewater rafting was lost until I recently found it again – one of the riches that had been stored in a secret place. Thank you for always seeing me and being with me. Now as I share the story for first time, I pray it will help someone else who is at the point in their life like I was on May 21, 1998, when I thought…

"I Can't Go On!

Me? Go whitewater rafting? I don't think so! I don't like water deeper than my bathtub, and I definitely don't like the water to be churning. Yet, there I was, watching the guys unload the rafts. I sat on the steps listening to the guide tell me about falling in the water. My biggest concern was that I would be in the part of the raft that was least likely to put me in the water. But I listened. He was telling us that when we fall in (not if) to swim the direction the guide had said was the way to safety. He told us that when they threw the rope we were to put it over our shoulder and lay back in the water and they would pull us in. Because, if you are facing down the water will rush into you face and you will let go of the rope. There were other instructions, and I listened carefully to all of them. **I DON'T WANT TO GO IN THE WATER.** (I don't swim very well.)

The raft was ready. The life jacket was on. I was helping carry the raft down the steps to the water. As we started down the river the water was peaceful and calm. The guide was going over the instructions again. I listened, again praying that I wouldn't fall in the water. We were approaching the first rapids. My stomach was churning a little. In just a few seconds – splash – I was in the water. My eyes were open, and I saw cloudy water. I was experiencing *fright.* I surfaced and tried to get my bearings. The last instructions I heard was that I could only depend on myself to get safely out of the water. No one was going to come in and get me. My brain was quickly trying to process what I needed to do. Suddenly I saw that my guide was in the water too and I somehow made my way to him and grabbed him. He tells me to swim. I'm so frightened I don't think I can. The water pulled us apart and I was alone again. I was frantically trying to remember what to do. I remembered I was told to lie back and let the water carry me. I tried to relax and do that. When I did, I saw the raft, and I saw the people in it getting the safety rope ready to throw. My hand shot up from the water and before I knew it, I had the rope, and I was being pulled to safety. I was hauled into the raft breathing fast and shallow. I was frightened to the bone. I kept saying, "I can't do this. **I can't go on!**" I want to go back. I was being assured that I was ok and to take deep breaths. I was told it hadn't been my fault that I fell in. It took a couple of minutes for that to sink in and gave me the courage to say that I would go on and not quit. I was still very frightened, but I wanted to keep going.

We were in calm water again. I heard the safety instructions, but as we approached the next rapid, I announced that I was really scared. I kept paddling and kept listening to the instructions of the guide. I made it through that rapid still in the raft. *Okay,* I think, *I can make it.* Another period of calm, then the next rapids are announced.

Because I am actually on a training run the instructor is talking to the guide. I hear about 360's and about not hitting the big rock and I tremble in fear. We navigated the rapids again and I was still in the raft. "Is the worse part over?" I asked. "No," came the reply. My fear is subsiding but each time we enter a new rapid I paddle hard and loudly say over and over, "Lord, don't let me fall in the water. Lord, don't let me fall in the water."

I was not as nervous now. I was understanding how to ride the waves and not fight them. There was still the possibility of going into the water, but the joy of riding the waves was getting stronger than the fear. Sometimes the other raft was in front of us and I could see them ride through safely and that boosted my confidence. The guide and the instructor reassured me that I was doing well. Now I was relaxing during the calm times instead of spending all my time dreading the next rapid.

We finally reached the place where we left the water. I *almost* wished it wasn't over. But as I left the water I was filled with a sense of pride and accomplishment. I could easily have quit after the spill, but I would have missed so much.

I thought about how this experience mirrored my life. Life had knocked me in the water when Wayne committed suicide. I struggled and became frightened. Then, I started to hear the voice of my instructor and guide, the Holy Spirit. He reminded me that I didn't have to be afraid or fret. He reminded me to trust. I surfaced, I got my bearings, and I saw my Savior standing there with the rope ready to throw to me. My hand shot up, I grabbed the rope, and he pulled me to safety. I rode along in the calm for a while, then, I saw more rough waters ahead. How was I going to go on without him? I started processing what I had already learned, and I was able to keep paddling and ride the waves. I began to enjoy life again and saw the rough places as opportunities for God to strengthen me. I knew that at some point, as I continued to follow him and his leading that I would be in the water again. But each time I would be more prepared. I was not as frightened, and I was learning new things. I was learning that as I prepared to make a major life change, moving halfway across the country by myself, that fear didn't need to stop me.

Other things happened during my trip. My guide had not come into the water to save me; he had fallen in at the same time I did. How like God to put someone else in the same situation just when I needed help. The guide also benefitted from my experience, he was learning valuable lessons that were going to help him do a better job that summer, and the others in the raft were getting more experience helping to rescue the perishing.

When I returned, I found my pastor, the person who was responsible for me even going on the trip, and I said, "I thought you liked me." He laughed and assured me that it was just part of my adventure and something to write about.

CHAPTER SEVENTEEN – THE EXCAVATION CONTINUES

You will keep the mind that is dependent on you in perfect peace...
Isaiah 26:3

Remodel or Renovate

My husband, Felton and I have now been married fifteen years and enjoy watching home improvement shows together. Each show wants the same outcome, to take a house that needs some TLC, work their particular brand of magic on it and turn it into a show piece. Fixer to Fabulous, Unsellable Houses, Good Bones, Home Town, No Demo Reno, are just a few of the ones you can find on HGTV. On some of these shows the homes are renovated. They are given a fresh look, personalized, and updated. Other shows do remodels. The functionality of the home is improved. This could mean room designs are updated or it might mean a new layout that better suits the owner's lifestyle.

My *Good Christian* box needed to be remodeled. It didn't just need a new coat of paint and some wallpaper. It needed a demo day. There were still lies attached to that box. I still believed I had to be perfect and the fear of failing, fear of being wrong, and fear of what others would think had come with me. My box needed a Romans 12:2 remodel "...be transformed by the renewing of your mind." Colorado was going to be the perfect location to start.

218

Excavating this time in my life showed me that God had allowed me to be in the perfect place to heal. Because I didn't know anyone and no one knew me there were no expectations about how, when or where it was okay to grieve. I didn't have to worry about other people's happiness. There wasn't anyone I needed to rescue and as far as I could tell no one was judging my choices and decisions. However, there was a downside. I was alone.

I would go out for a walk every day and enjoy the beauty that surrounded me. One day as I was walking, I thought, *You don't have any form of identification with you and if something were to happen no one would know who you are or who to contact.* I wasn't in daily contact with anyone at that time so it would take a while for me to be missed. Another time I went to Walmart and as I was walking across the parking lot I thought, *There is no chance that I am going to run into anyone I know.* Those two events exacerbated my loneliness.

The people at my new church were extremely friendly and it wasn't very long before I had a couple of dinner invitations and some friendships developing. One in particular, God used to help remodel the box. She invited me to lunch one day and by the time lunch was over we had bonded. We had similar back stories, and we were at the same place in our spiritual journey. We had been believers since we were children, but we were still spiritual babies. Our friendship led us into a deeper walk with the Lord. Proverbs 27:17, "Iron sharpens iron, and one man sharpens another." She became my accountability person. If I couldn't call her and tell her what I was getting ready to do I knew I shouldn't be doing it.

Six weeks after I got to Colorado my son was getting married, so I made a trip back to West Virginia. That was a very difficult trip. Wayne was supposed to be Nathan's best man, and he was in spirit. It was a beautiful wedding. Family, friends from church, several of my college friends and former co-workers came and surrounded me with love and support during those days.

I was still on disability when I moved. As I got settled into my apartment, I was feeling pretty good so I decided it was time to see if I could go back to work. You are allowed a three month trial work period on disability so I started with a parttime job at one of the ministries that was located in the Springs. I wasn't well enough to work full time, and I couldn't live on the parttime salary, so I had to quit.

I still needed some supplemental income so I did something I never intended to do. Before I left West Virginia I had attended a Mary Kay event that was designed to recruit new consultants. When I filled out the survey at the end of the event the level of interest in becoming a consultant that I marked said, "I'd rather eat grass." I had signed up as a consultant for personal use only, so I already had the supplies I needed to get started. It served the purpose of some extra income, but the bonus was the friendship that developed with my director.

In April of 2000 I realized that my health had improved, and I was going to be able to work full time. A couple of days later I got a call from my friend who told me about an opening for a bookkeeper receptionist at the Christian radio station. I sent my resume, and even though I had no formal bookkeeping training I convinced them I could do the job. From that point on my Myasthenia Gravis was never a problem. If you google the question, "Is Myasthenia Gravis curable?" the answer is no. God had chosen to heal me.

I was physically healed. My heart was much better and spiritually I was growing. My *Good Christian* box was being remodeled and I wasn't even aware. There had been a few times at work that my "I have to be perfect" lie showed up.

What I've learned is that when I was not perfect and was criticized, constructive or otherwise, I would immediately hear my shame attendant say, "you are incompetent." While the lies hadn't been completely refuted, they seemed for the most part to be dormant while I was in Colorado.

So What?

Heavenly Father,

As I reflect on the last four years of my fourth decade I view it as a time of healing. A rest from the relentless lies of my shame attendant and a time of real growth in my relationship with You. My shame attendant continued to torment me with my body shame. I went back to Weight Watchers. However, when I look at pictures and see the weight on my weigh-in booklet this had more to do with my pride than my health. Weighing and measuring and keeping track of my food kept me obsessed with food. The bathroom scale kept me obsessed with body shame.

It was a joy and not a chore to read Your Word and pray and I was getting to know You better and better.

My writing continued. I started writing more poetry in response to lessons learned in Bible study. Those poems were collected and put in a little booklet that I shared with the ladies in my group and a few other friends. I found it in my treasure box and realized that it was the prototype for what became my first book.

My journal entry for this decade read, "Mom died, and Wayne took his life, and I moved to Colorado and you gave me a friend and I grew and grew in You, and my Myasthenia Gravis went away.

Thank you for the respite. You used it to get me ready for the next big event in my life. This time it was a happy event. I was going to be a Nana.

Loving You more and more,

Amen

CHAPTER EIGHTEEN – HOW HEALING HAPPENS

...and binds up their wounds
Psalm 147:3

Binding Up the Wounds

My mom was our neighborhood's "Good Samaritan." In Luke 10:34 speaking of the good Samaritan Luke says, "He went to him and bound up his wounds, pouring on oil and wine..." The neighbors would call for Mom and off she would go. She did things like put butterfly bandages on head wounds and give morphine shots to the neighbor dying of cancer among other things. She gave advice on how to bring a fever down and went to the neighbor's the morning they discovered their baby had died in the night from SIDS. She bound up the aching hearts of the parents. Our yard had a basketball court where all the neighborhood boys played so her skills were often put to good use. Not only did she bind up the neighbor's wounds there were plenty to take care of in our house.

When you entered our house through the front door you were in the living room. In just a few steps you could turn right into the kitchen and immediately on the left you could enter the laundry room. You could then exit the house through the side door.

On more than one occasion the sister in the house would lock the front screen door so the sister outside couldn't get in. Then the race would begin. The sister on the outside would run as fast as she could around the outside of the house to get to the side door before the sister inside could get there and lock that door, too. This particular day I was the sister on the outside. There was a two-step concrete porch at the side door. I tripped as I got to the porch and skidded across it on my bare knees. Remember that we always wore dresses, so imagine raw meat that definitely needed to be bound up. The wound had to be cleaned to prevent infection, then big white gauze bandages held on with white adhesive tape adorned my knees for many days while the wounds healed.

One thing the Good Samaritan in the Bible and my mother had in common was that they did not heal anyone. Binding up a wound does not heal it. It protects it from further injury and holds it together so it can heal. As I was getting ready to write this chapter, I made a discovery about the word wound used in the Luke passage. The transliteration of the Greek word is trauma. And in the Old Testament in Hebrew the word wound can be translated as pain, hurt, injury, sorrow.

I believe that God bound up every one of my wounds as they happened. He held them together as I learned and grew. Then when I was mature enough in my understanding of who He was and I was ready to accept His healing, He could take the bandage off. Sometimes I had to forgive those who had harmed me as part of the healing process. There were still scars but they were reminders that while I had been wounded, I had been healed.

In the months after I moved to Colorado, I started working on a book that had a working title of *Bandages for My Broken Heart*. I did a lot of study and research and much of what is in this book came from that research and the writing I did. As I considered the wounds I experienced during my life, I thought about the methods God had used to bind up those wounds. I found this list in the pages I had written 28 years ago. I am now able to see how these bindings helped me.

- Reading God's Word – Held me and guided me as I waited with hope for healing.
- The Holy Spirit – Was always with me and interceded for me.
- My family – Gathered around me when I was sick and when Wayne died
- Church family – No matter where I lived, I had the support of my church family
- Activity – Redecorating, traveling, rappelling, white water rafting gave me things to do and held me together many times.
- Counselling – Seeking guidance from good Christian counselors many times.
- Remembering – Reading old letters, looking at old pictures, traveling to see old friends, and all my friends who had offered comfort were salve on the wounds.
- Forgetting – Letting go of what if and if only.
- Writing – Journaling, poetry, articles, and a book.
- Reading – Books written by those who had walked this journey before me.
- Sharing – My testimony of God's faithfulness at church, at Christian Women's Club, and with friends and family.
- Moving – To Colorado to meet new friends and learn to use my pain to minister to others.
- Writer's conference – Where I found my personal mission statement – *To ignite in women a passion to get to know God with gut level intimacy.*
- Moving – To North Carolina to be a Nana and find new friends and publish my first book.

None of those things provided healing. God is the healer. He is Jehovah Rapha the God who heals. I found healing as I walked through the decades and wrote the "So What?" sections at the end of each chapter. That is where I was able to be transparent and vulnerable and look at my wounds in light of who God is. The more I read God's Word through those decades the more I could see His plan for my life. The more I read scripture the more I learned that struggle and pain and heartache are what God uses to conform us to the image of His Son.

All along this writing journey God has providentially provided just what I needed to hear at just the right time. I listened to sermon clip, posted on Instagram, of my nephew, Adam preaching. The title of his sermon was *Joy in The Journey*. He shared about his personal struggles while he served in the military in Iraq. He said, "And so now, even this week, I can look back on that situation, those circumstances, the horrible stuff I went through in Iraq, I can look back on it all and find some joy in it. Because no matter what I went through, I was still able to serve the purpose of God and preach the Gospel." That was Paul's goal when he was in prison in Rome writing to the church in Philippi about joy.

Talking about all the struggles Paul experienced Adam said, "If I was to go through something like all of this, I may start believing that I have gotten something wrong along the way; that my understanding of God's will was somehow flawed. Even that God was punishing me for something. We tend to associate negative circumstances with failure or punishment, don't we?" He went on to say, "Paul looked for the opportunities in whatever circumstances he encountered. Because he looked to God's purposes and trusted God to provide whatever he needed, Paul was able to focus on the Gospel."

Many times when I was struggling with Myasthenia Gravis those were my words. I would think, *I must have done something wrong and I am being punished.* My son remembers a time when he found me in my chair with my Bible open and tears running down my face. When he asked what was wrong, I said, "I don't know what I'm doing wrong." What a healing way to change the narrative to understand that the lessons learned in those struggles became opportunities for me to share the Gospel.

North Carolina

My first grandson was born in February of 2002. I made a trip to North Carolina to meet him. My accountability friend had a grandson who was six months older than mine. One day in September as I was watching him crawl around on the floor in his Nana's dining room I thought, *I'm missing this and I don't have to.* By the end of October, I had my condo on the market, and my U-Haul loaded one more time and was headed east.

It would take another book to share everything that has happened since that move; two more grandchildren, two jobs, marriage, and retirement to name just a few. What I have learned is that most of my problems and struggles during these last twenty years were the result of the wounds and heart break I had already experienced.

If you have a broken arm and someone bumps it the reaction is much different than it is if your arm isn't broken. I have learned that the same thing applies to emotional wounds. Trying to be good enough and please everyone left me broken and vulnerable to the bumps that come in relationships. When I was believing the lies I was easily offended by others and wanted them to change so they wouldn't bump my wounds. As the truth has healed my wounds, my relationships have been experiencing healing as well.

So What?

Heavenly Father,

There is so much to talk to You about as I finish this book. I want to start by saying thank You for walking with me through this excavation project. My hope for healing when I started this project has been realized. The bandages are off and the lies I was believing have been replaced with the truth.

The lie that my parents didn't love me has been replaced with an appreciation of them. Dad was a wonderful provider and protector who loved the Lord and served others well AND he didn't know how to nurture. Mom had a servant heart and used it as she supported Dad in everything he did. She was an example of the older woman described in Titus 2. She loved me very much and showed it in how she served and cared for her family AND we did not have a joyful, secure attachment.

The lie that You were disappointed in me has been replaced with the truth that You have always known everything about me and that You knew my heart, saw my struggles, bound up my wounds and carried me through some really dark days. You love me with an everlasting love. You chose the exact parents I needed to be the Rachel I am today.

The lie that I was defined by my body has been replaced by understanding that man looks on the outward appearance, but You look at my heart. The scale and mirror do not get to define my worth.

The lie that I had to be perfect because of what other people would think has been replaced with knowing that I am not responsible for what others think. I don't have any way to know what they think. I am to walk with You and learn and grow to be the woman You want me to be and don't have to have the approval of anyone else.

The lie that I am responsible to make anyone else happy by what I do and how I behave has been replaced with the truth. I am not responsible for their happiness.

I remember in one of my early Dawn sessions she drew an isosceles triangle that represented any situation that is causing me trouble that I want to change. On the bottom left corner, she wrote the words *power* which represented *authority*. On the bottom right she wrote the word *control*. At the top point she wrote *responsibility*. She explained that if I didn't have any power or authority in the situation, I was not responsible for it. And if I did not have any control over the situation, I was not responsible for it. Now many months later I have learned how true this is, and I have learned skills that will let me apply it.

Understanding how my brain was created and learning to be more aware of what I'm aware of has helped me recognize the lies of my shame attendant much more quickly. I recognize the lies because I've grown and spent so much time reading Your Word and meditating on the truth. Another benefit of doing this is my *Good Christian* box got completely dismantled because I'm not trying to follow a set of rigid and judgemental rules. I am following Christ's example.

John 8:32 sums it all up. "You will know the truth and the truth will set you free." And John 14:6 where Jesus said "I am the way the truth and the life…" The answers were always in the Bible. It took me a long time to read and learn for myself. I no longer accept that because I didn't have a prescribed "quiet time" I hadn't been learning Your Word. I now know that spending time with You through reading Your Word and praying is what builds that relationship. Paul wrote these words to the church in Galatia, "It is for freedom that Christ has set us free. Stand firm, then, and do not let yourselves be burdened again by a yoke of slavery," Galatians 5:1. **There is**

freedom in truth and slavery in believing and living the lies. Understanding that is what brought healing for my wounded and broken heart.

There are things I'm still learning how to apply and You keep providing me with new resources every day that help me handle things in a way that is more pleasing to You. Just like You promised I sought You and found You because I was seeking You with all my heart.

I could write another book (and maybe I will) about the sanctification process that happened to me during the next decades of my life. For now, I'll just thank You for what You did and how happy and free I am at this moment. Remembering Romans 8:6 will be my guide going forward. You used Paul to tell me that when my mind is set on my flesh, I will experience death; death to peace and joy. But when my mind is set on the Spirit there is life and peace. I'm learning to recognize when life and peace are in jeopardy to run back to You. I can also live my dad's life verse, I Corinthians 15:58, "Therefore, my beloved brothers, be steadfast, immoveable, always abounding in the work of the Lord, knowing that your labor is not in vain."

The journal entry for my 50-59 decade read, "You were there and good and faithful when I moved to North Carolina and didn't have insurance but You gave me a job I loved for nine years and friends and grandchildren and I grew and grew."

For my 60-69 decade I wrote "You were good and faithful when Felton and I got married and I was able to work through past hurts and some new hurts and learn how to be a good wife and lead lady's Bible study and become a missionary with Felton and I'm growing and growing."

Speaking of Felton, I'm going to stop for a minute and write him a letter.

Dear Felton,

Surprise! I waited until you thought we were all done to add this letter. I just wanted to let you know how much I love you and how much I appreciate how you helped my dream become a reality. The hours and hours of reading and editing can't be counted. You have made the book so much better.

It was at the end of my fifth decade that God brought you into my life, after twelve years being single. I thought I was just fine by myself and then you came along and changed all that. You are a faithful Christ follower who serves others like no one else I know. Getting to serve with you at JAARS and now doing life together during retirement has brought such joy. Our biggest claim to fame has been visiting all 50 states together.

Being involved at Mercy Church and watching what God has been doing also adds so much fullness to our lives. I'm excited to see what else God has in store for us in our future.

Thanks for loving me and always being there for me through the good, bad and hard times.

Love, Rachel

I'm back, You know I wasn't very happy about turning seventy. I told Blake, one of my pastor's, about how hard it was. He sent me a text and told me he had prayed that my 70's would be the most fruitful time of my life.

Today on my 74th birthday I recount what I wrote in my journal about the 70-79 decade. "May my seventies be the most fruitful years of my life. As you continue to sanctify me, I will sing of the goodness of God. OH! I will sing of the goodness of God."

THE END

Also by Rachel A. Bollinger

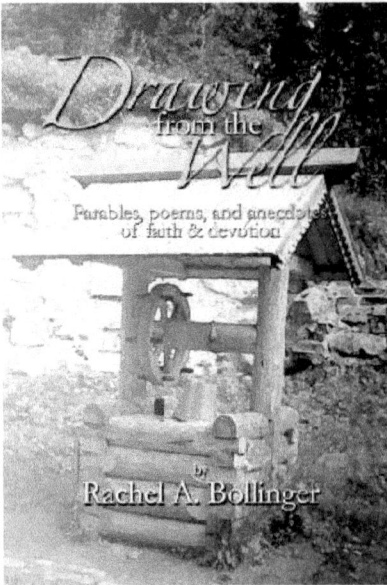

Drawing from the Well

A collection of parables, poems, and anecdotes to enhance your spiritual journey. Author, Rachel A. Bollinger walks you through her personal challenges and triumphs, referencing scripture and entertaining you as she walks closer to God. Join her as she draws from her well of experience, faith, and discovery.

https://tinyurl.com/2s44p8m6